LION COUNTRY

Mary Chipperfield

LION COUNTRY

HODDER AND STOUGHTON
LONDON SYDNEY AUCKLAND TORONTO

CONTENTS

KEY TO ACKNOWLEDGMENTS
1   United Press International
2   *Evening News*
3   *Daily Express*
4   *Antony Miles Ltd.*
5   *UPI Magazine Services*
6   David Robson
7   John Drysdale
8   *Daily Mirror*
9   Keystone Press Agency Ltd.
10   West Advertising Ltd.
11   BOAC

ILLUSTRATIONS

I

Once upon a deer park

*I*T ALL began with a dream that came true. My father, Jimmy Chipperfield, had had an eccentric vision of lions roaming free in England, as they had not done for over a thousand years; and he had had the guts to get his scheme off the drawing-board and into the countryside. The first fifty royal, tufted-tailed, carnivorous quadrupeds had been let loose in a fenced deer-park in Wiltshire, and motor-cars were about to move among them. It was an experiment that had never been tried before, in this way, anywhere in the world; the consequences could be disaster or glory; there was no way of telling which.

The Chipperfields were in equal partnership with the Marquess of Bath in what was known as the Lions of Longleat project, and the truth was that we were all riding a tandem along a tightrope at a great height, with a vast number of people on the ground gleefully predicting a mighty fall. Together with my husband, Roger Cawley, I was totally responsible for the day-to-day running of the Longleat reserve, so our hopes and fears were as strong as any.

On the brink, we were all greatly heartened by the arrival, one spiky February day in 1966, of a helpless golden ball of spotted velvet, all big, deep eyes and pink-orchid mouth. It was sad that his twin had died, and that his lioness mother had rejected him. But this our cub was alive, though only just—the premier Lion of Longleat and England's first stately wild cub, free born in a west-country manger to parents from East Africa. Breeding and conservation were what my father's experiment was about. This was a notable beginning.

Inevitably, the little fellow, who weighed less than three pounds, was christened Marquis. At once, I took him into my heart, and into my bed at The Pheasantry, our animal-dominated home adjoining the lion park and just half-a-mile from the Elizabethan splendours of Longleat House. As I told in *Lions on the Lawn,* Marquis needed all my care for a time; but he not only survived; he grew to lithe grace, beauty and intelligence such as I have never before found in an animal.

Now, almost two years of daily adventures have passed, and we take up the story with Longleat reserve an enormous success and totally accident-free; with my father righteously justified to the point that almost every other stately home in the country wants his lions; and, even more important to me, with Marquis roaring his pleasure at having reached lionhood.

My 'baby' was now three hundred pounds in weight, nine feet from tip to tip, and capable of breaking my neck with a mistimed swipe by a forepaw. But what I thought of most was that he was on the point, perhaps, of repaying the love that had been lavished on him by fathering English lions as fine and handsome as he.

When an animal is hungry, I notice instantly; if he is sick, I read the signs in time. So it is with sex. Even today, the world seems bent on making a neurotic mystery out of a simple process. That's what comes of cooping millions of people in concrete jungles. They lose the way. Country children are surrounded by uncomplicated creatures doing their things; they see sex in the fields, the hedgerows and the cowsheds, just as they see and smell other natural functions taking place. 'So *that's* how it happens,' you observe when you're three or four, on witnessing a coupling of beasts, and then you forget all about it, except as a part of what goes on in the seasons, until you are in your teens and it is your turn—your need.

Marquis was in his teens by the closing weeks of 1967, and, when his voice broke, he lost no time in showing me that he was ready for a lioness.

It was no moment of high drama, or anything. I was strolling from the kennels to the stables one frosty morning early, when, as I passed my tethered friend on the way, I said to myself 'Ho, hum! We'll have to do something about that erection of yours, won't we, Marquis?' And, as lions are naturally polygamous, I started casting around for a couple of suitable feline débutantes for so mighty a prince—feeling for all the world like a marriage-arranger in the Far East.

As soon as I had groomed my horse, I slipped Marquis's chain and led him by the collar, across the cattle-grid by the entrance to the yard, before allowing him to lope free by my side along the brittle woodland margins until we reached his favourite corner of the estate, with its kidney-shaped pond, sheltered by trees, shrubs and reeds, where together we slithered down the bank by the pollard elm, grunting our pleasure at the happy outcome of the chase. The green-glass surface had begun to freeze around the edges, but nothing short of plate-glass ice could keep Marquis from his dip. In he plunged, roaring and splashing, among the coiled lily roots and spongy weeds, as I sat laughing on the drystone wall and thinking, 'Well that wasn't exactly what I had in mind for curing your new condition, but it'll do for now.'

As always, when he came out, Marquis shook the water off his long thick coat, all over me (for lions are dogs in many ways,

rather than cats) and settled with a yawn on a carpet of leaves
and twigs by my feet, idly looking into the rippled water for a
sign of the ancient pike which inhabited the deep end of the pool,
as we listened together to the lion choir in the reserve across the
way.

But it was not the usual nature lesson, or a quiet drinking-in of
fresh air, as we sat by the pond this morning. I had more important matters to talk to Marquis about. Wagging a finger to
command his full attention, I explained my plans for his future. I
would have a good look around the reserve, I promised – pointing
towards it – to see if there were any surplus females, of sufficient
beauty, who were unattached. But I counted this most unlikely, I
explained. The four large prides were settling down so unexpectedly well that to withdraw any lioness could do harm at a
crucial time. Not to worry, though, I added. There were some
absolute corkers among the new young lionesses about to leave
our quarantine stations at Southampton and Plymouth, and I
made shapely signs with my hands, grinning the while, so that
he knew he could trust my judgement in the matter.

If you think me odd in talking to my lion friend in this fashion,
I can only chide you for missing out on an important and pleasurable aspect of this life on earth. I tend to the strong-and-silent
approach, as far as human beings are concerned, but I happen also
to believe it is beneficial to talk freely to all other living creatures.
If you welcome the first tiny green shoot to appear in the bowl,
your bulb flowers will grow straighter and more beauteously;
chat up your rose bushes as you pass and they will bloom more
abundantly; sweetly chide a fruit tree that is slow to blossom
and it will prove that late crops can be great crops. Birds, too,
respond joyously to daily social intercourse, and we are visited,
by our fireside, almost nightly, by a lonely little field-mouse who
drops in for a chat, and pricks his ears at any praise we offer.

After all, didn't Winston Churchill disclose that he was

wont to divulge 'secrets I could tell no man' to a favourite poodle; didn't Colette reveal the 'unmentionable' dark side of her life to sundry pets and thereby obtain solace; and weren't Somerset Maugham's dachshund, Erda, and Guy de Maupassant's cat, Misti, loving to their masters in a wife-to-husband way?

Such relationships can be bizarre (as with the jackdaw who courted her master by taking him ritual offerings of food, and stuffing these in his ears when he covered up his mouth and nose) or sadly ridiculous (as with the budgerigar who lavished every mark of tenderness on a ping-pong ball after her bald master died) but they can also be as splendid as they are real, and such had long been the way with Marquis, to whom I now went on to explain that he had been singled out to help produce a strong and definable English strain of bright and robust lions, so he would have to stay with 'mum' for a bit and enjoy his harem within easy reach of the house.

This was something to which I had to give some urgent thought. Up to this moment, to everyone's concern but mine, Marquis had been sharing my bed when he felt like it. It was a symbol of the perfect trust and understanding between us. He knew it and I knew it. Father, on the other hand, was furious (assuring everyone that in a long life, he had never heard a tall tale like it—only this one was true!) and Roger (who had to trot Marquis down to the garden to relieve himself the moment he woke) was not over-amused on cold mornings. Otherwise, Marquis lived around the house or in any old outbuilding that suited at the time.

Now, attractive quarters would have to be found for the young sovereign and his child-brides, where their all-important nuptial nights could be checked upon. There were plenty of adaptable outbuildings and we had lots of labour around the place to do the work. So, as we walked home, I went on to outline this part of the plan and to explain that, although he would thereafter have a place of his own, I certainly was not shutting him out of my life or my room; he would still be welcome when he felt like it. The choice would always be free.

A quick trip to Southampton a few days later resulted in my being able to sort out, from the many possibles, half-a-dozen probables for the Marquis Beauty-Queen Stakes. But before I could study them as carefully as was necessary, we were thrown into a fever of activity that put Marquis's sex needs into the background for a week or two.

The B.B.C. had been dickering for some time with the idea of doing a 'safari' series at Longleat. Now, suddenly, they made up their minds to go ahead, and we were inundated by executives and technicians. As the series was to be about the reserve, I did not think I would be too much concerned in the detail, but I agreed to accommodate the producer so that I could help and advise him in the early stages.

Inevitably, this delightful chap, whose name was Derek Burrell-Davis, became so bemused and besotted by life at what some wag called 'the lions' corner house, that he passed more time following me around than he ever spent in the reserve. In a Press interview, he explained thus: 'When I reached Mary Chipperfield's home, where I had kindly been given a bed, I walked into a scene that would put such Hollywood hokum as Daktari to shame. The house is called The Pheasantry, which is a big joke because almost the only creatures not to be found within its walls are pheasants. Noah's Ark would be more appropriate, except that a lot of the animals go about in threes and fours instead of two by two. There were at least thirty animals of one sort and another around the outbuildings, including a fully-grown African elephant in one of the garages. I had to ease nervously past a large tiger, lounging in the yard like a watchdog. Round the corner, a black panther was chained to the front door.

'Inside the house, the scene was even more incredible. Two baby gorillas and a chimpanzee were taking turns at pushing

Mary's year-old son in a wheelbarrow; there were lion cubs in every room, including the loo; a young tiger was going up the curtains in the sitting-room like a squirrel; a baby leopard was asleep in the larder; there was a sinister python tied up in a sack under the kitchen table; an old donkey was shoving its head in the back window; and there were cats and dogs everywhere, including Sean, a Great Dane, Henry, an Old English sheepdog, Yula and Gipsy, Alsatians, plus Winston and Brandy, the St. Bernards, and tiny Amy, a schnauzer, who was liable to be squashed to death at any moment by some heavy foot, but always seemed to survive. There was also a fully-grown lion walking about with Mary. It could have swallowed her down in a snap and two gulps.

'The first night, I crept downstairs to the kitchen to get a drink of milk, only to find the panther (a sinister-looking beast if ever I saw one, about the size of a large greyhound, but stronger and plumper) propped against the 'fridge, asleep. Fortunately, it did not wake when I gently extracted the milk-bottle. The next morning, while I was having coffee, the tiger came up and started playfully chewing my arm until someone called it off. I was thankful for the thickness of my jacket.

'I then discovered, to my astonishment, that all the animals were house-trained and had the free run of the place. Indeed, the Chipperfield–Cawley household proved so engaging and enchanting that, although all the programmes were supposed to be about Longleat, I there and then decided to devote half of them to The Pheasantry, because the whole set-up was so natural and marvellous . . .'

So it was that for two or three weeks, late in 1967, I became deeply involved in television, as did Marquis and my other animals. In all, thirty-five crew were mixed up in this expensive and exhausting operation, but I do think the results justified this. Certainly no other British television series can ever have been anything like this one. In all, four programmes were filmed under

the general title, *Doorstep Safari*, and they went out in due course
on Sunday afternoons. Marquis ran through his many routines
with such facility that I was extremely proud of him; I took
Suki, one of my fully-grown tigers, for a swim; we had a chimpanzee tea-party, with David as the guest; my twin bears did
their tricks in a fountain, and so on. This was all incidental. The
programmes, rightly, had a serious side to them, and each one had
a chat-show type of discussion in which we threw about various
ideas and problems on animal raising, behaviour, danger signals
and so on. But the filming in the reserve was to prove the most
fruitful in the end.

There had been no problem for the camera- and sound-men
over my trained animals; in all cases, I am the boss; while they
enjoy their routine performances, or they would not do them, they
are never in any doubt that they must implicitly do what I
tell them; any naughtiness is instantly punished—usually by
banishment or loss of privilege—as a child would be punished
in similar circumstances. And the great thing to know is that,
no matter how long or how well I have known a wild animal,
watchfulness is still absolutely necessary at all times. If an
animal is within striking distance, I never take my eyes off it for
a second. I deliberately demonstrated before the cameras what
inbred savagery is like in the raw, by pretending to be about to
take a piece of meat away from my friend, Marquis; much as he
loves me, he must never be disturbed when he is eating; he went
for my gloved hand instantly, and really meant it. If my timing
had been amiss, I would certainly have lost an arm in front of
several million viewers.

Most of this is predictable stuff, within the framework of
unrelenting vigilance over creatures whose characters are known to
me intimately. But most of the fifty lions in the park are unknown
quantities to me as far as behaviour is concerned. I know them all
by sight, and can name each one; I am also acquainted with their

At the Christmas lighting switch on ceremony in Warminster,
December 1967

Suki wishes Mary luck on her wedding day

superficial personalities, in the way one knows one's neighbours. But, in the absence of disciplined training, I would not dream of taking the tiniest chance with any of them. They are unpredictably 'wild' (just as mine are unpredictably 'tame'). There is a vast difference, as I warned the producer and his crews.

We at Longleat had already proved (through the stupidity of a small proportion of visitors) that many of the lions, male and female, will attack the moment they see anything unusual. They are accustomed to cars moving through the reserve with closed windows; that is 'normal' to them. But let one driver wind down a window in the sight of the more resentful pride-leaders and a great hairy paw would be reaching for the occupants almost instantly if the wardens did not intervene.

Inevitably, therefore, life was very different for Derek and his Wood Lane wizards in the lion park from what it had been at The Pheasantry. Applying father's admirable principle that there will never be trouble as long as the people are locked up and the lions are free, we shut all the crews in cages or put them up towers and cranes. This worked very well until some of the absent-minded artistic types involved forgot themselves and left their 'hides' to answer a call of nature, or to make a 'phone call, or for some less obvious reason. Quick though the wardens would be in all such cases, the lions were never slow either, and several not-normally-athletic B.B.C. types must have set several new A.A.A. sprint records as they hared through the grass towards the outside broadcast vehicles. Derek, the producer, himself sampled long-hair-raising incidents of this sort more than once. And out of his own experiences was born a great idea.

One day, during the two weeks of night-and-day filming, after Derek had been on the telephone to London even more than usual, a pantechnicon arrived in the yard and disgorged a dozen very life-like dummy figures of women, men and children. Dressed elegantly in Saturday-outing togs, these had been made up

B

specially at the props department, and were wisely filled with kapok, indicating that one, at least, of Derek's talks with me in The Pheasantry had not gone unheeded.

I guessed at once what he was up to, and I was right. An old car was secured and placed near the reserve entrance, its roof-rack stacked with 'luggage'. While Mike Lockyer, our chief warden, with armed assistants, kept the inquisitive pride-chiefs (who had quickly detoured to approach against the wind, as a matter of course and of instinct) at bay, we towed in the car and grouped the dummies around it like a typical 'forgetful' English family who had hopped out for a moment to see the lions better. Derek's aim was to find out what would happen if the 'white hunters' were not ever-present as shields between the beasts and the public.

The armed men then withdrew, with astonishing results. The instant Mike and the others were fifty yards or so away, the lions attacked, instantly and viciously, closely followed by their mates, and with a few cubs in close attendance also, learning the ropes; no sound but a series of swishes announced their coming; once astride their victims, however, they uttered respectively short, menacing, quivering 'grrrs' of satisfaction, and puppy-like squeaks of appreciation. For an instant the air was full of clouds of cotton wool and flurries of jacket-arms, trouser legs or dummy heads, as the mighty beasts snapped and tore at all the 'human' figures. (In conversation, I had told Derek foam rubber could catch in the lion's throat and choke it—hence the kapok). Only when there was no trace of blood for them to lick before the feast did the leaders get bored, and with them the followers. There was little left of substance, anyway. They then turned to the roof-luggage which they viciously tore to shreds, with equal ease, while old Atlas had a go at the rubber tyres, as he was wont to do, howling his pleasure when one went pop and the air hissed **out.**

All the time, the cameras turned and the tape recorders whirred, their operators more pale than they had been at any time since they arrived. At the end, when even the cubs were bored with the sport, Derek turned to me and whistled his astonishment. 'My God, Mary,' he exploded, 'that could have been us.'

This short 'horror' film was extra to the series. It was shown nationwide and may have caused a bit of domestic toilet-hopping among the hundred or so visitors who, over the eighteen months the lion park had been open, had placed themselves, their families and our staff in positions of danger akin to that of the dummies in the film.

All in all, the B.B.C. series did some good, and this 'extra' may even have helped to prevent 'incidents' and accidents. What we have been attempting at Longleat is as real as it is earnest, and that's the impression the films gave. We want people to learn from their day out, as well as being entertained. By contrast, most of the nature or wild life programmes I see on the 'box' are about as remote from reality as it is possible to get, and therefore tend to do harm by giving totally false impressions of animal behaviour. Usually, they concern some noble white hunter being saved by animals from the villainies of other humans; or a Tarzan-figure fights a group of carnivores single-handed before becoming the leader of a tribe of grey elephants; or a vet performs an operation on a 'friendly' lion without drugging it first. It would be dangerous if it wasn't so silly.

The latest American animal-caper we had tuned into had featured the villain being knocked unconscious by a blow-back of poison from a dart-gun; he was then trussed in a net by a baboon, and then dropped into the Atlantic from a helicopter piloted by a chimp. At least, this episode made us hoot with laughter. Life at The Pheasantry was much less exotic.

There were Christmas lights to be switched on at Bath and Warminster. In the former case, the ceremony was duly performed by the Marquis and the Marquess, and the highlight was the lighting up of a forty-foot tree Lord Bath had felled himself for the occasion.

Afterwards there was a celebratory cocktail party in the mayor's parlour, at which guests were promised the treat of sharing their canapés with a fully grown lion. No-drinkers both, we had been to lots of these do's together before, and knew the drill: wait for the grub to come up, get it down fast, and then scarper gracefully. On this occasion, I could barely wait; the nippy night air had made me ravenous.

But Marquis was moody for once, as well as magnificent. It was past his bedtime, for one thing, and he had been irritable for a couple of days anyway. Almost at once, he squatted on the carpet of the dimly-lit room, impersonating one of his cousins in Trafalgar Square, and nodded off grumpily. But the deep-piled carpet was exactly the same colour as the lion's skin, so that once or twice short-sighted old dears, on their way to the next large gin, fell over him and were nearer their maker than any of them could have realised. Marquis's mouth was now so cavernous, it could almost have accommodated a brace of them in one go. Reluctantly, because of my hunger, and fearful of the outcome if we remained, I quietly led the cross lion to the car park and we drove home grouchily under a tall sky that was frostily licking its stars, as if they were acid drops. For once, we scarcely said good-night and Marquis indicated he would sleep in the byre behind the stable.

At Warminster, things again got out of step. We were on our own, and Marquis was asked to press the switch with his paw. The resultant flash, and the dazzle of lights, upset him somewhat, to the point that he sulked and had to be disciplined, as he was led in procession through the town with Santa Claus. Again, without our supper, we headed for home. This time, I must have shown weariness or displeasure, because, as I drove towards

Longleat, a huge head came over the seat and rubbed against my ear, to be followed by the sandpapering of my face by a tongue so large and rough it could have been a pink loofah. Not for the first time on such journeys, I nearly put the safari-wagon in the ditch.

I suppose there are unhappy phases, like these, in the best-balanced relationships, when friends fall out twice in a row without really knowing why. But such tiffs were so rare as to make these quick-fire ones disturbing. Normally, any outing with Marquis was tremendous fun, as well as being essentially an adventure. Maybe, on these occasions, he had been bitchily getting back at me for delaying my promise to arrange his betrothal. 'Beggar that for a game of soldiers,' I muttered, when it dawned on me that this was probably the truth and that his irrational conduct was stemming from nothing more than adolescent frustration. It was rather silly, and I lost no time in telling him so. I had only one pair of hands and a large 'orphanage' to run, apart from the many other calls upon my time. He had my assurance I'd fix things the first moment I got. Meanwhile, the one who should have complained was Roger; I was so tired at nights, I scarcely remained awake long enough to collect a good-night peck.

Part of the reason for this was a long run I had had of night-feeding deserted cubs from the reserve. The first few days are critical enough, especially if the baby has sucked even once on its mother; but, having got one, or a litter, past this stage, there comes the long haul of building their strength, via a bottle of powdered milk every couple of hours, night and day, and subsequently at longer intervals. Only a one-woman band maternity-home matron could have any idea of what this is like. There have been many weeks over the period when I have had five or six 'babies' all at different stages, according to age, and all getting different strengths of milk or other foods. And each cub, with the new quarantine laws putting up their value all the time, was worth two or three hundred pounds to the Chipperfield–Bath organisation, as well as the kudos that would be handed out internationally for successfully rearing so many; so I kept going somehow, not wanting to lose any 'babies' because I needed sleep or food or anything like that! As I've said before, when Jimmy Chipperfield is doing the animal-stocktaking, good husbandry is of the essence.

So I told Marquis off and he took it very well.

Then, before any of us realised it, the carol singers were swinging their lanterns on the back porch and the frost was back with a vengeance.

Animals know about Christmas, as anyone who has pets around the house will tell you. Indeed, many of them respond to it with more sensitivity and enthusiasm than children. They feel instantly the excitement of the preparations and the steady build-up of tensions towards the shared pleasures of the most festive day of the year.

When I was tiny, Christmas was still old-fashioned enough to be centred around children—and in the circus, where the family is all, we had some marvellous parties. There are, or at least there were, few delights for a child as great as the electric thrill of little hands reaching to touch a toy-bulging stocking in the fat darkness before the dawn; and in a caravan, it was all somehow more romantic than it has ever been in a house.

We sang the old carols, like 'See, amid the winter's snow', or 'By night on wild Judea's plain', and they meant something awesome to us, for weren't we travellers and shepherds, stoically sheltering our precious few animals against all that Nature could throw at them? And when we went to the candle-lit carol services, so simple and moving in the west country, and heard the stark purity of the biblical message, it, too, had its echoes in our young hearts. 'And there were in the same country shepherds

abiding in the fields, keeping watch over their flocks by night . . .
and they were sore afraid.'

We had been poor, and cold, and sore afraid, on many a
dark hillside, listening only to the sounds of our 'flocks', and
wondering if the next day's circus would be well-enough
attended to pay the farmer for the use of his field. Faith had been
necessary, not once but half-a-hundred times. Faith had invariably
paid off, and somehow or other, each time we had been able to
stride forward once more.

It all seems so long ago, and yet I cannot fully believe that those
days of pure childhood have gone for most of us, never to be
enjoyed again.

Hardy has written of the ox and the ass on their knees in the
stable on Christmas Eve. This I have never seen, but all animals
certainly know that the Lord's birthday concerned and concerns
them as well as people. It is therefore as important to make all
domestic pets part of the festivities as it is to involve the rest of
the family.

Marquis had arrived in the world a little late for Christmas,
1965, but he had certainly made up for it last year, so that I
only had to speak the word to him and he remembered. 'Marquis,'
I said, 'it's Christmas!' Scotsman-like, Marquis gave his usual
deep gruff grunt of acknowledgement. 'Uuuuuumph!' he went,
his tufted tail swishing approval, and a distinct grin hovering
around his huge fangs, as he cocked his head to hear more.
'Uuuurrrmph!' he concurred, and his great body trembled into
purring.

The other word he wanted to hear at this moment was 'toffee'.
So, I told him 'toffee', and he nuzzled me, in response, with such
rough affection I almost fell over; all tiffs were forgiven and
forgotten.

The story behind this was that on a mad impulse, at Christmas, 1966, I had decided to make a largish quantity of treacle

toffee, using one of those marvellous big, old-fashioned brass jam-making pans. The gob-stopping brown 'goo' had turned out so well that the family had chewed and crunched at it for days, which was reward enough. But Marquis's response had been more unexpected. Like all lions, he dislikes sweet things; failing fresh brisket of Englishman, give him a nice juicy ox-head any day, to gnaw on for an hour or two, and maybe a bit of rib on Sundays. But, unpredictably, he had shown great interest in the smells produced when I was boiling up the brew; and he had unexpectedly accepted the first sample, which I had hardened in a saucer by the open window, to sniff at inquisitively and to push around with his forepaw. I had made it; he was happy to investigate it and play with it.

All that Christmas Eve, and most of Christmas Day, that simple saucer had given him pleasure; there was something about the smell of its contents and the noise the saucer made, as well. Mind you, I'm sure part of his lionship's somewhat sardonic-seeming pleasure initially was *surprise* at seeing me actually cook something in the kitchen. I'm not what you might call a domesticated woman. I never ever played with dolls as a child (live animals being much more fun); I cannot sew or knit; and cooking only interests me to the point of briefing our cook on how many people are likely to be sitting down to lunch or dinner.

So, first of all, I'm sure it was the shock of seeing me with a pan in my hand, food ingredients on the table, and a general air of Fanny Craddock-ish kitchen showmanship that Marquis found such a knock-out. Then his nose told him that what I had produced could be pleasurable to the nostrils, too, which made the event doubly memorable.

Now it was toffee-time again, except that the clock was creeping around to midnight on Christmas Eve before I found a moment to dig out the old pan and clean it. By this time, Roger had been called out to investigate a scrap between lions in one of the huts on the estate; Marquis was lying watching me from the warmth of the kitchen range; and the cubs were snug as salted snails in their baskets, having tired themselves out climbing the Christmas tree and miaowing for help as they got wrapped in the decorations. I was glad of Marquis's attentive company in the now-still night, as I dug out the ingredients, rolled my sleeves up, and sloshed some water into the pan, as it said in the forgotten-for-twelve-months recipe.

I then added the demerara sugar, put in the cream of tartar, treacle and syrup in correct quantities, and fidgeted while I waited for the mixture to come to the boil 'to a temperature of 300 deg. F. or' (Marquis please note) 'until, when the mixture is dropped into a saucer with a little water, it should harden instantly . . .'

Thinks: 'There are too many things still to be done for me to stand looking at a pot of treacle in the hope that it is really climbing the Fahrenheit scale with one hand behind its back!'

So I hopped it, for a few minutes, into the pantry, to prepare some raw minced beef for the older cubs, only to be brought hopping back again by what can only be described as a deathly scream from Marquis, accompanied by the sizzle and smell of what I'd call a noxious burning substance!

Of course, the molten mess had reached its boiling point with ease, and had risen evenly to the top of the jelly-pan, whence some had spilled on to Marquis's mane, while some more was doing a Mount Etna dance on the hot plate. At a glance, I saw that Marquis was cowering, mainly unharmed, in a corner, pathetically acting the scalded cat, nursing his injured dignity and pawing a solidified sticky mess stuck to his tawny top-knot; I also saw that there was still a gallon or so of the gooy stuff ready to erupt from the pan all over the cook's clean kitchen.

But not for nothing was I the fastest draw in the cowboy-and-Indian act in the Circus. In one movement, I grabbed a cloth and used it to swing the pan, with its contents, off the stove; scarcely pausing, I turned another forty-five degrees, and emptied the entire mess into the sink.

Yes! You've guessed it! The toffee ran down the drain, where it met the requisite quantity of cold water. It promptly crystallised beautifully, hardening like granite and jamming the entire plumbing system.

Please allow me to draw a veil over the rest of that Christmas Eve night, except to say two things: (a) Marquis was very big about it all and allowed me to take the pinking shears to his splendid mane (as the only means of getting rid of the goo); and (b) the plumber, when he arrived, turned out to have no sense of humour, but I was by then sitting on the floor laughing hysterically enough for ten of us and wishing a dozen awakened miaowing cubs a Merry Mary Christmas.

2

Tout ça change . . .

On the brink of his fulfilment, let me try to set in perspective my relationship with Marquis.

Almost from babyhood, we all search for a special friend with whom we can share the more important intimacies, cares and joys of the passing day: not someone we meet once a week for a gossip and a giggle, but someone we can be with, in person or in spirit, all the time. Such rare friendships are generally to be found (if they are to be found at all) outside marriage and outside the family. In that way, they are extra special.

Marquis, my monarch of the wild, is that kind of friend to me.

He found his strength in me when he was little more than a bag of bones, with a tiny one-stroke heart, but it is not from that springboard that our relationship arose. After all, I'm the girl who has lions like other people have rabbits; I have since hand-reared a couple of dozen equally-appealing cubs (and many other young animals) without going weak at the knees about any of them. Marquis stands out for me like an alp in the plains of

Syria. He exudes the sort of calm strength that lifts me up when I'm down, that gets me going when I'm lethargic. He has a presence, a style and a stature that are irresistibly all his own. He's only got to look at me and I feel good.

This does not diminish, threaten or alter my relationship with Roger, my husband, which is as happy and complete as any girl could desire. It's just that (in my birth-sign and in my feelings) I'm half-animal, half-human. I have therefore sought the ultimate in animal companionship, as well as the ultimate in human companionship, and I rate myself extremely lucky to have found both. Let me put it this way: Roger and I are opposites, which is usually the best possible way to be in a marriage; Marquis and I are twins, which can make for the closest of friendships.

As far as the facts are concerned, almost as soon as the bluish film had gone from his baby eyes and he could focus them, Marquis chose me for his lifelong friend. I knew it then, as I know it now, and I welcome it, for the inner strength it gives me. Not only that, but he'd fight for me against any odds, as I suppose I would for him.

Mind you, it's not all ESP and animal magnetism. I've got as shrewd an eye for a superbly muscled beast, and for the speed of its mental responses, as I have for a handsome, intelligent man. As a girl born in a circus, it's second nature to me to weigh up physical attributes, brains and style. And Marquis, as well as being my special friend, is a sort of animal Sacha Distel-Weissmuller.

He is also uncomplicated, and that is a marvellous quality to find in anyone. There are things in life which are beyond words, beyond intelligence, even—things which only instinct can reach; these things I can sometimes attain with Marquis. We squat together, regarding the teeming world of nature, and, suddenly, aspects of it seem simpler and more beautiful than before. I throw a problem at Marquis and, without words being spoken, it comes back into my mind solved. You don't have to believe this, if you don't want to; the important thing is, it works. And if *he* needs anything, as was currently the case, he does not even need to ask.

In the animal world, as in the human world, it's example that matters most, and we both understand that; we'd rather be *doing* something than planning it or thinking about it. Mostly, we find it better to arrive than to travel.

As soon as Christmas and New Year were over and the visitors had departed—the visitors who seemed to descend on The Pheasantry in greater numbers than were arriving to see the animals or the big house—I lost no time in calling in skilled labour from around the estate. Quickly, I had one of the larger outbuildings strengthened and made comfortable for Marquis's harem-home. As he had been sleeping in all sorts of strange corners over the holidays, so as not to frighten the guests, I think he was doubly delighted to move into permanent quarters, albeit alone for the time being. 'This is your very own place now, Marquis,' I repeated, 'and your brides will be with you by the end of the week.'

A few days later, when I felt he had settled-in happily, I took a safari wagon to Southampton and held the finals of the all-important beauty contest. Three of the contestants (for the prince's paw) were too attractive to resist—sleek, plump, quick and outgiving—so I decided that three brides for one lover would not be too many in the circumstances.

As it happened, the 'girls' (who would be aged thirteen to fifteen in human terms) had been given at birth the appropriately regal names of Lady, Vicerene and Countess so they must have been outstandingly beautiful babies, too. In theory, the proposed unions seemed to promise an idyllic and productive set-up, but I never forget Rabbie Burns's strictures about 'the best-laid plans', so I would just have to wait and see how the four would react to each other, and how they would interrelate. The fact that the three young lionesses had shared a cage, in the bed-sit land of quarantine, without fighting, gave me some reason for hope. But Marquis's reactions to them would be the decisive factor. There is no Women's Lib in the lion world; the male is supreme master; his will is paramount in all matters, from food to sex; and the wishes of his wives can only be dealt with after he has obtained his satisfaction.

I had done my best for my friend. These lovely and coquettish creatures would have had their names in lights in Leicester Square if they had been around when *Born Free* was filmed; Lord Rank would have selected them instantly, in earlier days, for his Charm School. In a phrase, they had the lot. But I could only trust to instinct that Marquis would even see them that way. Many animals are totally irrational, by our standards. For instance, they apparently attach excessive importance, in judging one another, to the sort of smells the telly is always telling us to suppress. What if these three had the wrong sort of niff, and did not turn Marquis on, solely for that reason? In failing to sniff around the lionesses, had I failed him in his most important request?

I had arranged with Roger that Marquis would be chained up in the office, out of sight, scent and sound of his new quarters, at the time I would be returning from Southampton. I was therefore able to let his three brides smell his smells and pace out the dimensions of the den before being faced by their lord and master. I remained with them for a time, closely watching their faces and bodies for signs of fear, anger, curiosity, jealousy, and the other postures animals can exhibit in moments of change. Predominant in all of them, I noted thankfully, was a suppressed excitement, triggered by the whiffs of Marquis's 'Old Spice' the straw offered; they showed their physical reactions to this by pawing at the straw and by low whines of interest.

The next move was to let the dog see the rabbit, as it were. I had no intention of setting Marquis loose among the young ladies until they had had time to settle properly, but it was important that they should look upon each other every day, meanwhile. The new quarters lay about a hundred yards from the house, beyond the cold store, but, as I led Marquis across the garden and into the yard, I was astonished to find that he could already sense the presence of the lionesses and was difficult to restrain. So I stopped, made him sit, and gave him the whole bit again. The days of his fulfilment were at hand, and I would hide nothing from him; but patience was of the essence.

As soon as I was sure he realised we were mainly going for a walk (which would fortuitously take us past the girls!) I led him to the lion-proof, floor-to-ceiling, chicken-wire, viewing window the workmen had fitted into the front of the building. When he saw the lionesses for the first time, Marquis stopped instantly, his whole body alertly trembling with excitement. Then he began to utter the sharp but suppressed yelping sounds with which lions indicate interest in each other. It was a very good beginning.

I then led him fairly close to the netting (at which point the yelping was taken up by the females) and let them all briefly look their fill before taking Marquis back to the gate for his normal constitutional. Throughout the introduction, he had behaved magnificently. I think he sensed my fears that he might disgrace me in front of the lionesses and the workmen who were still around. So he kept his cool and, in silence, allowed himself to be led on up the path; in silence, too, the lionesses watched him go, guessing, as females can, that very soon he would return. It was a beautiful afternoon, and my heart was singing. I was not losing a son, as the saying goes, but was gaining three daughters.

There were, of course, those who would see things differently. Twisted minds can be depended upon to raise twisted theories at almost any excuse, don't you think? The simple answer is the last one they ever want to hear. The zoological world is not a large one, so my dalliances with a fully-grown lion had not gone unnoticed. There were many theories on offer to explain the situation. One of the printable ones was the laughable idea that, in looking at me, Marquis was imprinting on my form the image of a female lion—as mother, wife or whatever. What tripe!

This 'imprinting' is supposed to happen to animals who are treated over-possessively by humans. Whether it ever does or not, surely only the animal can say. In my case, I may have been calculating to Marquis (which *is* my nature) but I was never possessive (which is not *me* at all).

Sometimes I think there are as many theories around about animal behaviour as there are animals. Mostly I only listen if there is something in it that could be practically helpful in solving a long-standing problem; and even then, I'm suspicious until I have tried it out for myself. For the rest, I find that there are few behavioural tricks that a good old-fashioned application of affection or of suitable chastisement cannot eradicate.

Anyway, now that he had suddenly grown up, and was about to leave 'home', all such silly theories would have to be revised. The simple fact was that Marquis had never ever shown the slightest signs of being neurotic, least of all now. Rather, he had a wicked wink in his eye, which is how things should be between friends— and I felt like saying 'Trousers for lions!' or something daft like that.

Here was a normal, well-balanced, uncomplicated down-to-earth lion, treating the transition to sexual fulfilment as no more troublesome than his earlier switch from milk to minced meat. I only hoped my little boy, David, would do me as proud when the time came.

The one thing that can prevent healthy lions raising healthy

Kumar enjoys his egg and milk in the kitchen

Playing with four-year-old Marquis

Don't look now but . . .

Marquis sits nervously on Jarro for the first time

offspring is if they are unhappy. If I had anything to do with it, Marquis and his mates would be the happiest collection of lovers in modern times. I was now as concerned about the quality of their offspring as about anything then in prospect in my life. Calculating, did I say? Mercenary Mary, too, might fit!

These were some of the thoughts that had invaded my mind as we trotted the wintry paths of the estate together, our mingling, short-panted breath made manifest in the icy air. I had decided on a different route today, for no other reason than that it was something of an occasion. It was possible to take Marquis along routes in winter that were denied us when the visiting traffic was heavy.

On this occasion, we loped past the road by which the coach traffic for the reserves reaches the estate, turned left at Stalls Farm, and bounded on down a path towards the north end of Half-Mile Pond, the elongated lake where visitors board replica Georgian barges to feed the sea-lions and to see the 'wild' adult chimpanzees on Man-Ape Island. We're open every day of the year, but this was the middle of the quiet season and today, a murky Monday early in January, around the turn of the year, the crowds had been thin to the point that most had by now gone home.

As we neared the hippo pens, I could hear the subdued sounds of Arnold and Freda making love, and I marvelled again at the unexpected tricks nature plays, such as the fact that these ex-tremely bulky beasts can utter the most unexpectedly meek sounds when mating, as indeed can those other monsters, the rhinos.

The frost had eased slightly and the lake was free of ice; other-wise Marquis might have been able to share another astonishing sight I had witnessed once or twice over the years—the two hippopotamuses doing their own ice-breaking in order to go swimming. That's another thing. Before we opened at Longleat what was to be the world's first safari park of this kind, the critics almost *all* said our African animals would never survive

c

exposure to the English winters. In fact, the sun-raised hippos absolutely revel in the varieties of weather they are offered; the lions, too, are even more lively at Longleat in cold spells; the imported ones adapted, in the first place, during their year in quarantine at Plymouth, by growing thicker coats; and the English-born cubs, given vitamins with their food, soon adjusted similarly, and, never having known anything else, imagined our climate to be 'normal'.

Generally speaking, indeed, the critics could have saved their crocodile tears for some more worthy cause than our 'hothouse' animals and their move to 'refrigerated' Britain. The truth is that all animals are in constant conflict with nature, wherever they may be living. And they always win because they adjust.

As we came in sight of the house, and a wider vista of the grounds, I could not help thinking what an incomparably magical setting it was we and our animals lived and worked in, even in winter. The estate occupies ten thousand lovely acres in all, mainly in Wiltshire. There are seven hundred acres of parkland and about five thousand, eight hundred of woodland—mainly softwoods, such as Douglas fir, spruce, Lawson larch and oak; ash and beech are predominant among the hardwoods. In season, the azaleas and rhododendrons make a great spectacle. In addition to exotic wildfowl, peacocks and golden pheasants, the herons and house martins are equally praised for the flying spectacles they provide.

Longleat House (first completed in 1580, and long known as 'the treasure trove of the west') does not, like so many country homes, hide behind a screen of trees. From the main gateway, which we could now see, the drive swoops down, as straight as an arrow, to the front door, a mile across the park, and with every yard the traveller realises with a thrill that he is looking on a perfect jewel, a magnificent early Renaissance mansion with ninety rooms and a window for each day of the year, expertly set in a bowl amidst the beauties of the low Wiltshire hills. The name of Longleat, by the way, comes from the Half-Mile Pond, set in the 'long leat' or 'leet' of the river or stream near the house, dammed by the brilliant gardening-artist, Lancelot 'Capability' Brown, who so splendidly planned the estate grounds in the eighteenth century. Lake birds include a variety of ducks—Pintail, Mandarin, Carolina and Mallard mainly.

That the native fauna had its adjustments to make was underlined as we jog-trotted on along the winding edge of the lake, near where the gorse was spitting yellow spikes, and shiny-plumed traveller's joy, unobserved was climbing the bleak hedges, where even the tired holly's greens and reds seemed to have shrivelled. Suddenly, the comparative calm was broken by a flapping of wings out of the darkening sky, where the sun was barely holding out its white arms before drowning in cloud. The flap was caused by a pair of whooper swans arriving from the north (as they tend to do in winter) and soon they were trumpeting noisily at apparently having found a clear stretch of water to call their own. But the resident mute swans—which, legend has it, must never leave Longleat or the Thynne family will die out—were only dozing in the undergrowth. In a flash the mutes, who may not be able to trumpet but who are certainly not deaf, took to the water to defend their stately pond from this undignified exhibition of noise and commotion. Unceremoniously, they drove off the incomers, with a great deal of haughty wing-thrashing and aggressive posturing. Marquis would have been in there, helping to scatter the intruders, had I not held him back. There was nothing he liked better than a game of 'chase me, Charlie', which he obviously thought this was.

Torrential rain had started to fall, out of the blue, so to speak, and was pasting my long hair across my eyes like a poultice; we were far from home and in line for a thorough drenching; it served me right for varying our route so radically. I galloped

Marquis across the grass to the Wisper Bike Circuit next to the Children's Amusements' centre, when I 'phoned to Roger and asked him, please, to collect us in one of the Land-Rovers. English climate, did I say? It is always harder on the natives than on the foreigners! Whereas we never know what to expect, *they* know to expect the worst!

There were fewer and shorter walks for Marquis later that week. I had begun to spend more time with the lionesses, talking to them in their quarters and pointing out the various animals around their area, partly to get them used to the new environment, partly to charm them into a cheerful condition, and partly to observe better their maturing bodies. Thanks to these sessions, it became apparent to me on the Saturday that Lady would be the first to come on heat, and I was very relieved.

With dog bitches, you expect this condition twice a year, spring and autumn, and can prepare for it; with cats you can reckon about every Tuesday and twice on Sundays; but with lionesses in England, no accurate pattern had yet been settled. On the experience I had had, it could be anything up to six months. So I was having to use my eyes and my intuition, lest I missed the opportunity to cash in on what looked our most promising breeding arrangement. For the observant, the signs, when they do come, are no more difficult to observe in a lioness than in a cow; the appropriate posturings, sidlings, attempted mountings and inviting noises are all part of the normal drill among mammals.

Lionesses also tend to snarl, swear and bare their fangs as part of the 'heated' performance, aimed at attracting attention. When I am feeling catty, I swear I can see *all* these symptoms in women, when my attractive husband is near, even when they are *not* on heat, but that's another story!

As a rough means of confirming Lady's condition, I led Marquis round the back of the yard, where the soiled straw from the harem had been temporarily dumped; whereupon he immediately went sniffing around part of it—presumably where Lady had placed her jets. Turning up his nose excitedly, grunting and chuckling, he told me he had read the message. 'Say no more,' was his summing up. 'This is it.'

'Big head!' was all I said, but my thoughts were busy enough. As the average lioness is on heat for only four days at a time, I now had to act fairly fast.

Leading Marquis around the awakening countryside, and watching him sniffing his way from puddle to post, I could not help reflecting how useful the nose is to an animal. He already knew Lady's smell and he would follow through, led by the nose, at the moment of maximum acceptance.

Yet in the superior world of man, true scents are suppressed and false ones substituted; we make a fetish of 'nice' smells, such as after-shave, flowers, old books and log fires, and condemn anything as natural as body odours. It's all a sort of perverse duplicity.

Double-dealing and dishonesty do exist outside man, but not all that much, and usually purposefully. Animals rely on smell so much that they can be fooled by nature herself, as, for example, when an orchid entices wasps to pollinate it by manufacturing and discharging the same smell-trace as the wasp itself secretes.

But it took man, with his sophisticated deceitfulness, to think up the idea (which I recently saw demonstrated at a farming show) of squirting a sow with essence of boar, from an Aerosol can to make her arrange herself in the mating posture—although all she got for her trouble was artificial insemination!

The Longleat lions will be developed without any such sophisticated nonsense—you can be sure of that.

Anyway, as soon as I got back to The Pheasantry, I called out Roger and my brother, Richard, in case I had misread the signs to the point that there should be a jealous and costly fight among

the females; then, with an affectionate slap on his flanks, I set
Marquis loose among his brides. There was quite a stir for a few
minutes, as he weaved in and out of the three lionesses, executing
elaborate figures of eight, as they crouched and cowered, moaning
convulsively, overawed; then he singled out Lady, by the same
process that he had used to find the message of her jets and we all
withdrew to leave them to get on with their honeymoon in private.
To the men, it was just another coupling arrangement, successfully
begun; to me it was an end and a beginning.

3

And robin came too . . .

I'D LIKE
to say I found it difficult to sleep for the next few nights, what
with Marquis enjoying his honeymoon only a hundred yards
away from the bedroom where he had spent at least one-third of
his young life; but the truth is that I had far too much else on my
mind for any such extravagances. There were cubs to feed
several times per night; and even on the fourth night, when the
mating phase was over, I had other anxieties. These mainly
centred round Hereward, my pet snake (you dig? Hereward the
Wake—I mean Snake); my mother had telephoned from South-
hampton to say that he would not keep his food down; she had
given him fresh young rabbits, in the hope they would please
and settle him, but up they had come. She did not know what to do
for the best except send for me.

I had had Hereward, an Indian python, for about ten years,
and had presented him in several commercials and films, so I knew
his fads and fancies; he would only act this way if something was
worrying or frightening him; I would need to go south as soon
as possible and see what was wrong . . . wrong . . . wrong . . . Zzzzz!

I seemed only to have been asleep for minutes when a commotion began in the outhouse where Marquis had been in residence for three nights with his young bride. In a flash I was out of bed, while Roger slept blissfully on: he has a capacity for 'fiddling while Rome burns' that I often feel I could strangle him for.

I would not have been surprised to have had disturbances on any of the previous three nights, and, had they come, I would have kept away, for, when a lioness is on heat, a lion will have intercourse with her as often as thirty times per day, and it would be as foolhardy to go near Marquis or Lady then as to try to steal meat out of their mouths at mealtimes.

But now the heat period was over. I had noted this fact the previous afternoon, but had not approached the honeymoon quarters, preferring to leave them for an extra night to cool down. So whatever was wrong, it had nothing at all to do with the mating process. Hopefully, Lady would now be well and truly served and uninterested in sex for many a long moon; certainly Marquis would be satisfied he had fulfilled himself, and would be peaceable again, in his sated state, and so would be approachable again, which I had intended to prove in the morning.

But *not* as early in the morning as this!

There are various sounds that lions make to express a fairly wide range of emotions. The one I was hearing now—a short, menacing 'grrrr' of alarm—was accompanied by sharp yelps of fear: a combination I had seldom encountered before. Something very unusual was going on, and the sooner I got there the less chance there was of it getting out of hand. Without even looking out of the window, I got dressed quickly and dashed downstairs, grabbing an old silver-mounted circus crop and a torch on the way. I threw open the french windows at the back, and was nearly swept against the adjoining radio-telephone control panel.

Dawn was lapping against the bleak stone-age landscape of the winter night, but while I had been asleep snow had piled in drifts around the house and a menacing wind was sweeping straight in from the Arctic and blowing flurries of the white powder into the office. Quickly, I slipped on my thigh-length rubber boots and an oilskin to continue my dash to the harem.

In a few five-league strides and a time of about eleven seconds, I reached the wire netting of the converted garage, and peered through. There were Marquis, Lady, Countess and Vicerene, crouching in corners, ears back, nostrils dilated, whining, yelping and growling by turns. All were sweating, either from fear, exertion, or both. At first, I could not see any reason for the state they were in, and, thankful that they all seemed safe and well, was wondering if I had been unfair the day before to the behaviourists: could this be some sort of post-orgy 'trip' the lions were having that I had never encountered before? Instinctively, I spoke sharply to Marquis and he raised his head from floor level, whining, but otherwise ignored me, his eyes (like those of the lionesses) fixed on the far end of the building.

Then the dawn light began to brighten by the second, and not sparing Marquis's feelings, I simply had to roar with laughter, as my eyes focused on the cause of the trouble. A little robin was fluttering pathetically against the far wall, his red breast-feathers bedraggled, his little thin body all a-quiver.

I knew at once what it was all about—this conquest of mighty African lion by tiny British bird—hence my helpless chortles. We all have peculiar phobias. As I explained in my last book, mine is an irrational fear of insects. Marquis's, which I had observed all summer in the hedgerows and ditches, is an obviously painful emotion aroused by any really *small* creature, be it rodent or bird. Somehow the weeny robin had found its way into the shed (maybe looking for a suitable future site in which to set up home, in late February or early March: such out-buildings being natural choices for their nests) and had been spotted by the nocturnal lions before he could escape. No doubt Marquis had first tried to capture this frightening little red devil (assisted by the ladies)—hence the sweat. But robin's speed in evasion would only serve to increase the terror of the four big 'babies'. When I got inside and saw the extent to which the bird had evacuated its stomach down the wall and beneath it, I realised that it must have been something of a traumatic ordeal for Mr. Robin, too, to be suddenly chased around a garage by four full-grown jungle cats like these. Closing the door and speaking calming words to the lions, I somehow managed to cup my hands over the exhausted little fellow first time—guile winning where strength had failed—and carried him past the bemused beasts to safety.

Having seen young robin safely off into the winter wonderland outside, and having vowed to put out some fruit, seeds, berries and fat on our bird-table as soon as I got back, I returned to the boudoir to make sure no harm had come to my charges. It was then that I perceived some further tell-tale signs, of great importance, totally unconnected with the bizarre happening of the past half-hour.

As I fondled Marquis's neck collar and talked to him soothingly, my eyes were on Lady, confirming in detail what I had briefly noted—that her marmalade coat and slender legs were scored with congealed blood from scratches she had suffered in the night; there were also bite-marks amid further scars on her head and shoulders.

'Well done, Marquis,' I said softly, as he began to purr. 'Very well done, old chum.' Biting and scratching are the normal, and apparently pleasurable accompaniment to the climax to the successful act of love in the lion world, an act which will generally have been repeated many times in a single night.

This cruel element in love-making is present in many species (and is not entirely absent in humans) and it reaches ridiculous heights in a number of cases, such as the preying mantis, in which the female will excitedly and enthusiastically bite the head off her partner while the rest of him goes on making love to her.

Already, Lady was settling down to sleep and certainly not complaining about her treatment at Marquis's paws (and fangs). The chances were that the siring had been successful. We would just have to wait and see—sixteen weeks being the required time-interval before a possible Son of Marquis might be expected to arrive.

Meanwhile, I looked at Marquis questioningly and said 'Walk?' There was no need to say it twice. The great lion yawned, stretched, drew his lips back over his teeth, and padded swiftly towards the door. When he saw the extent of the snow, he paused, but only briefly. Then we set off together, my gloved hand on his shoulder, to explore the great wide, bleak, naked fields, and the freaks of wooded frost beyond them.

Within seconds our rapport was again complete. Marquis's relations with Lady had been an experience for him, but it was also an experience apart, to be taken when necessary, with any of the three lionesses. It had no bearing whatsoever on his outings with me or on our continuing friendship; indeed, if repeated too often, it might become boring, whereas our adventures together were 'new every morning'.

Rooks were blowing across the fields, like charred scraps of paper in the wind-currents above a fire, as we trotted, heads down, into the driving snow. An old man, shuffling slowly towards one of the snow-capped cottages, in the mysteriously deceptive pink half-light snow sometimes brings, at first appeared to our eyes to be a gnarled and frozen wayside oak, advancing on its roots.

Bucking, snorting, and blowing like whales, we bowled on down lane where the only things showing above the snow were knobbly-jointed, wind-crippled thorns, and suddenly, round a corner, a pheasant bobbed across the white carpet ahead, bowing the while like a drinking duck, and disappeared into a garden, head thrust forward from white collar, for all the world like a curate on his rounds. For once, Marquis ignored the chance to kill and retrieve the bird; perhaps Mr. Robin had halted this habit he had had since he was young.

Breakfast at The Pheasantry would not be pheasant today, but it would be ready by now, whatever it was, so we about-turned for home, wondering on the way, at the frozen spring by the roadside—huge, like a swollen flower—and leaving Nature's crystal kingdom to the venturesome car-loads of visitors that were already rolling towards Longleat.

The first to greet us as we walked through the back door of the house was Tomasina. I say 'greet' us; actually he swept past like a grand duke, with other things on his mind.

Tomasina starred in a film named after him, and co-starred (didn't you know?) with Rex Harrison in *Dr. Dolittle*, and has never forgotten that he is therefore a little better than the rest of us. He is an old gentleman now, as well as a grand one, but, in many ways, he still rules the roost at The Pheasantry.

It was appropriate, in a way, that we should meet Tomasina so soon after the robin episode, for he was another robin in a way—an example of a small creature that inspired fear in larger ones. In this way, he could be a character straight out of *Tom and Jerry*, because all the dogs are afraid of Tomasina, like the big, cowardly bluffers they are. If he passes them in the yard, they keep their eyes shut, pretending to be asleep, as a cover for their cowardice. He moves through them delicately, with a certain style, flicking his tail occasionally in derision. Only when they are sure it is too late for a fight to happen do the dogs stir themselves and feign aggression.

Cook has long been a sucker for Tomasina. There will always be an extra saucer of milk for him, between meals, in the kitchen. This is usually hidden under the sink and cook has been known to keep watch, conspiratorially, while running a tap to cover the sounds of the cat lapping up the creamy milk in the secret darkness among the scrubbing brushes and pails.

Anyway, I did not forget the little robin, who had so amusingly enabled me to confirm the strength of Marquis's reproductive urges. Indeed, I raided the kitchen Tomasina had just left even before I had my meal, and put out a variety of tasty bits, not forgetting seeds and fruit.

There was a well-made bird table in the garden of The Pheasantry when we arrived, and I suppose it would have been heresy, anyway, to ignore the birds when occupying a house which once owed its existence to game-bird cycles. So, although I have more than enough to do in other directions, I try to feed the garden birds fairly regularly, as a sort of discipline of gratitude for the pleasure they invariably give me. It's fascinating how they can tell the time, and how they are always hanging around the table, whistling, coughing, fidgeting and stamping their feet, for all the world like young soccer fans in a queue for F.A. Cup tickets!

I tend to chide some of them, as I do my young animals, for rudeness and aggression at meal times. Generally, the greedy starlings are the principal bully-boys of the queue (with the chaffinches hanging back, despite the superior rank bestowed by their chevrons—their corporal's stripes—rather like diffident soccer season-ticket-holders); but the various tits can be cheeky, and the yellow-beaked blackbirds certainly lack modesty and delicacy, except in their sophisticated taste later in the year for young strawberries, or raspberries, or currants. The degrees of excitement among the assorted species vary according to the food I put out, which varies from day to day and may include fat, bread, bacon rind, cake, cheese, seeds and corn. The great thing is that—thanks partly to the wild state of our semi-neglected garden—a bird sanctuary-in-miniature is being created which offers endless interest and enjoyment to the family. No conductor could ever find a choir (no, not for a million pounds) to match the dawn chorus of the birds we still have in profusion, thank God, in the west country.

When Roger takes my place (in feeding them) our feathered layabouts generally head for the nearest cover and watch apprehensively, or cry out in fear, until he has retreated into the house again. This makes me howl with laughter, but he tends to take it as a personal affront, and sulks for a bit until one or other of the animals or children chats him up and takes him out of it.

Generally speaking, all garden birds totally ignore my wild animals after a time, just as they are unafraid of humans they know. I often take Marquis with me when I put the food out and it makes little difference to the clucking anticipation, the joyful flying around my head, or the final rush to be first on the table. Marquis is mainly bored by birds out of doors, except when I draw his attention to an unusual one and tell him about it as I would a child, although he does not like it when—as sometimes happens—they land on his back, in pursuit of an insect, or because he happens to be a suitable airfield at the time.

In Marquis's natural habitat, of course, the larger birds would be in danger of being killed and eaten by him when he was hungry and larger prey was absent, but he had never known hunger and the birds had never had their instincts for flight roused by the sight of a wild animal desiring them.

The so-called laws of the jungle are little in evidence at The Pheasantry or at Longleat, partly because they do not exist anywhere as strongly as the writers of adventure fiction would have us believe, and partly because our animals never have to wonder where the next meal is coming from. One of the commonest reasons an animal acts aggressively towards another is that it is hungry. There is no emotion involved in the kill: a raging need is being satisfied, but the act of killing is not inspired by anger but is coldly calculated. To fill the belly is the prime daily preoccupation of all wild creatures, great and small, and they will soon let you know if you forget this fact, even for half-an-hour.

One of the questions posed in the B.B.C. television series of the month before had been whether we should go the whole way in our 'safari' parks and allow our wild animals to seek, kill and eat their own game before the 'caged' watching public. I have no basic objection to this whatsoever. I hate the sort of English hypocrisy that says 'it doesn't matter what you do as long as you don't do it in the streets and frighten the horses', and I therefore dislike the attitude which says 'it is all right for the lions to kill their natural prey as long as they do it in Africa and not in front of our children'.

We created the first of these reserves (and now have them in a great many places in Britain and overseas) in order that families could study, photograph and learn from the creatures of the wild in safety and at leisure. Indeed, Longleat was quickly accepted as the unique showplace of England for the breeding, study and conservation of African wild life: not merely a spectacular place of entertainment, but also an educational centre in a magnificent historical setting, featuring more than one thousand unusual assorted animals and birds. Trouble has been taken to show the various specimens dramatically in quantity (i.e. in herds and groups) because in this way a stronger impression is imprinted on a person's memory than by seeing one or two examples of the species (e.g. in a zoo). The public knows all too little, really (with children probably knowing most when they are young, and then forgetting a lot of it) about the difference between the lower animals and ourselves. It is important not to rush and confuse people; the way in which our reserves have been created encourage visitors to inquire, find out and think for themselves— which is surely the most profitable educational method.

Nobody knows for sure how many private zoos there are, al-though the very thought is frightening. All a would-be zoo owner needs is planning permission from the local authority. After that he is free to proceed as he sees fit. Where our security arrangements are (voluntarily) elaborate and comprehensive, his may be totally inadequate, because, perhaps, of shortage of money and/or a lack of know-how, or for any number of reasons. This, inevitably, puts the public constantly at risk. There is no licensing or inspection system, and no sign, despite our best efforts, of impending legislation.

Zoos apart, there is far more to safari park management than people realise. It is much more than a matter of simply finding a willing estate owner and popping animals into his land at so many per acre. Apart from everything else, lions are as pernickety as humans about the company they keep and it takes time for them to sort themselves into prides and settle down.

Selection of staff is as important as selection of inmates. Animal-people are a breed of their own. It's not so much a job as a way of life. Fortunately, even in the family, we have varied interests. Richard is mad about elephants; father has a soft spot for chimps; and with me it's horses and lions.

Inevitably, the zoo-world establishment, jealous, outsmarted, and losing custom, has accused us of 'commercial exploitation'. In fact *our* money all goes back into stock and into improving things equally for animals and customers. We really *care* about both, which is what matters (and what pays) in the end, is it not?

Everywhere in this shrinking world wild creatures are being shot, trapped or squeezed out of their natural territories by mankind on the march. In the course of our thoughtless and selfish trampling and fouling of our environment we make things more and more impossible for our animal neighbours, English and foreign. Some we destroy because they have glamorous coats, which we envy. Others we drive from their natural cover so that we can take over their living-space. Whatever the reasons, the

Charles and David

Lord Bath examines the first lion cub born in the Park at Longleat

Baby giraffes born in 1971 to two mothers within half an hour of each other

decisions and the moves, only man's voice can be heard, arguing the justice of 'progress'. The call of the wild is muzzled and muffled.

It is all too easy to think of these as remote problems, particular to far-away areas and unrelated to life in urbanised England. It may be a timely thought, therefore, that before the Industrial Revolution there were still wild cats, lynx, bear, beaver, bison, moose, wolf and lammergeyer in most parts of central Europe. But they were virtually annihilated by changes in landscape and agriculture; the building of factories, towns and roads; the construction of reservoirs and dams; the introduction of drains, pylons and canals; and the reduction of open spaces. And more recently even the most tenacious of our smaller native wild animals have been similarly threatened.

Every time a roadside hedge is torn down in the march of 'progress', the richness of rural life, in terms of complex, inter-related colonies of little furry mammals, is diminished and can never be fully restored. Stoat, squirrel, weasel, shrew, bank-vole, dormouse, hedgehog, hedge-sparrow and rat are driven from their ancestral homes by rapacious bulldozer and are scattered in the woods, if any woods remain, never to be seen again by perambulating humans in that area.

Nor is the filling-in of a country pond any less heartless than a seal-hunt. They may seem tiny, insignificant creatures—the moorhens, dabchicks, frogs, lizards, dragonflies, reed-warblers, tiddlers, tadpoles and other English water-dwellers—but the fewer places there are for them to live, the less heart they will have to survive and we shall all be the poorer.

What matters if the bee sucks not as long as we have Bingo?

Fortunately there are still a few areas of England, and the depth of Wiltshire is one of them, where the spread of the sprawling, suffocating plastic carpet of suburbia is making slow progress, where tuned ears can still detect the scuttlings of shy and timid

D

creatures from cover to cover, and where caring eyes can still take in honeycombs of bankside burrows in a free green world.

I cannot say better, in answer to our rivals' criticism, than that, in caring, we are creating a *more* animated scene than existed before we arrived. Native wild life is flourishing in our safari parks more fully than ever before; all our creatures, great and small, have settled down together in biblical harmony; and (to make a point by slightly exaggerating an astonishing trend in propagation of species) with any luck our rabbits will soon be breeding like our lions!

Incidentally, we spend a considerable amount of time and money investigating animal nutrition and reproduction; we shall also be financing comparative medicine, animal psychology and physiology in due course. It all takes time. But meanwhile, as a family (on the maternal as well as paternal sides) we have the genes of maybe fifty generations of showmen with the strongest instincts for and experience of animals, which is more than can be said for the 'aristocrats' of the zoo world.

We have also, by the way, become the largest dealers in wild animals in the world, turning over six or seven million pounds per year in this way, and this position was not achieved without considerable experience and caring; and it is partly due to our activities that B.O.A.C. now carries more animal passengers than human ones. We much prefer to trap our own animals rather than buying 'blind', or even from other known dealers. Nor do we just go out and round-up the animals at random. We study the area and decide where our prey can be caught most easily, with least disturbance to its chemistry and personality; we then persuade it to move there voluntarily. If, after a length of time strictly laid down by father, the chase-truck has not caught up with its quarry, we always abandon the chase, and we do not renew it against that particular animal.

At the base-camp corral to which they are taken initially, all our animals are kept quiet for a bit for adjustment and until they can be rid of parasites. The physical adaptation and calming down of wild animals in this way is a very important phase of capture, and can mean the difference between life and death for the more nervous of them. It also means that, because they are in excellent health by the time they reach our reserves here, they settle down that much quicker and better.

Anyway, back at the old homestead, on the day after the English robin almost ruined the last night of Marquis's honeymoon, the temperature had dropped even further below zero, and there were reports of sheep buried in the snow, and of crows worrying them; but the visitors kept coming, presumably to see how the lions were coping so when I let Marquis out for his walk it was his own pond that we headed for once more, and we decided to take Charles the Chimpanzee with us as a treat for his birthday.

Chimpanzees are like dogs in that, if they are reared without an opportunity to play either with their mothers or with other youngsters of their own kind, they grow up into social neurotics. And this also applies to little boys, of course. David was slightly younger than Charles so their friendship worked splendidly, as they had much to give to one another, and, being so different, became less bored than perhaps friends of the same species would become.

Charles, who is a fantastic show-off, but a good pal, was two years old that very day, weighed about thirty pounds and was about three feet high. He had been David's favourite playmate since my son was born. Every day they had happily shared any toys that happened to be in vogue, including tricycles, scooters and wheelbarrows. He wore his own style of hot-pants, long before they were popular, but he likes best to dress up in exactly the same clothes as David. This got to the pitch that if David fell and needed a bandage, Charles had to have one too.

Daily, after he has done his required stint at Pets' Corner, near the big house, it has become routine for Charles to join David for tea with the family. As David has been taught table manners, so has Charles, and on the whole he is astonishingly well-behaved, albeit destructive sometimes, biting and chewing anything that promises to give way to his strength.

His greatest pleasures in life are to answer the telephone and to practise typing. He can also be useful to me in that he is capable of holding a bottle for a young lion cub, a duty which he performs gently and lovingly.

Anyway, David was away visiting his grandmother, but would be back in time to help Charles blow out two candles on his fruit and nut cake. Meanwhile, Charles was lonely so we took him along for the fun, and I carried a bunch of bananas—his favourite food—to feed him with along the way as an extra treat.

Marquis and Charles (never Charlie, as the Press sometimes calls him in stories and captions) had always been good pals, to the point that, when younger, the long-suffering lion had often given Charles or David a ride on his back, so I was unworried about taking them out together, even on the coldest day of the year. When we reached the pond, I set them both on extra long leads and we all had fun making a slide on the ice across the bearing surface of the pond. After a while I got tired and sat on the powdery snow on the old tree trunk where I played in a desultory way with Marquis—the old game of his pretending to bite and worry my coat sleeve (with my arm in it, of course) and of my trying to get it away from him. It was a useful trick, for television or a film, so I did not mind practising it again; at least it kept us reasonably warm and gave us exercise.

Suddenly, I heard distant squealing human voices and leapt to my feet. I had completely forgotten about Charles, and, knowing this, he had sloped off quietly. I quickly secured Marquis to a tree (with profuse apologies) and ran up the hill as fast as the deep snow would allow. The sharp cries of visitors, from the

direction of the reserve approach road, led my eye towards
Charles and I nearly died laughing. There he was, crouching
behind the hedge at the roadside, bombarding cars, mini-buses and
pedestrians with snowballs. The sun had come out, the road was
becoming quite busy, and Charles had found a new game. The
astonishing thing was that about twenty humans had got out of
several vehicles to observe the remarkable fact of a chimp bombarding them with snowballs, and yet not one of them bothered
to return his fire. This the chimpanzee found boring long before
I reached him and he was quite ready, when I took his hand, to
go home to tea and games with David.

Lord Bath was waiting in the sitting-room when we got back
to The Pheasantry, and, after I had returned Marquis to his
little pride, as well as getting the birthday party going elsewhere
in the house, I was delighted to sit with the Marquess and talk
'shop'.

He quickly explained that an invitation had arrived from Lord
Montagu requesting attendance at Palace House, Beaulieu, by
anyone prepared to 'dress regally, or as a Head of State', at a ball
in honour of the centenary of the purchase of the south-coast estate
by Lord Montagu's grandfather. Naturally, with racing-drivers
on the invitation list, publicity for his much-visited Motor Museum
was not far from Lord M's mind in planning the event.

So, why not publicise our lions through his rival lordship's
kind invitation? thought Lord Bath, who is no fool when it comes
to attracting column-inches of Press.

At first, we threw about the idea of sending Marquis as The
King of Beasts, in the fairly sound belief that he would siphon
off interest from even the most exotically-dressed humans.
'Follow that', they used to say in music-hall after an animal act
had milked the sympathy and the applause!

Alas, on reflection, we decided that Marquis was getting a bit
big for a sustained appearance (which would undoubtedly be

necessary) at a ball. There would have been problems of taking him to the toilet in a strange and rambling stately home, and there was the recurring problem that, when people have had a few drinks, they want to show off and 'handle' a lion which, although he had always behaved well in all circumstances to date, *could* be fraught with dangers.

Then came the idea that Lord Bath could cause quite a stir (in terms of originality and impact) if he attended, dressed in a lion skin, as the King of Beasts. 'The problem is where to get a suitable skin in the time, unless we sneak up on one of the more seedy specimens in the reserve and remove his coat when he's not looking?' he lamented.

'You must be joking,' I replied, very seriously. 'We've got everything.'

And we have. Apart from a selection of fine skins made into rugs, on the sitting-room floor, we have others around the house—including lions, tigers, leopards, and panthers. Lest someone accuses us of encouraging the slaughter of valuable and beautiful animals, to succour the fur trade, let me say that not only do I prefer to have my fur coats walking about around me on four legs, but also all the skins we have accumulated are those of animals we have owned and which have died for some reason or another. This should squash for ever any suggestion that I am soft-centred or sentimental. I love my animals while they are here, and remember them sometimes when they're gone. But their skins are both valuable and beautiful, so I would not dream of burying them in them, or burning them, or anything like that. If Marquis dies before I do, his splendid coat will undoubtedly be cured and placed in front of the fireplace or in some other commanding place in our home. Sometimes when I'm showing people around now, they get quite nasty, or catty, about the animal rugs we already have. Among the milder comments was one the other day, when a female said: 'What did this one do, Mary? Bite you too hard?'

So it was that a splendid lion's skin and head were dug out of our collection and fitted to the cheerfully-willing Marquess of Bath, and a coronet was placed on top of the lion's head. The total effect was quite startling and laughter-provoking. Maybe it was not quite as dramatic as Marquis, the lion, would have been, but it was generally judged to be more original and appropriate than the costumes worn by most guests (who included Diana Dors as Hamlet, Stirling Moss as a 'pearly king', and at least eight portly peers all impersonating Henry VIII, led by Lord Montagu as Charles I).

We got our wish. Longleat got as much publicity out of the event as Beaulieu!

4

Roger the tiger-hearted

*I*N DUE course, to my abounding joy, Lady showed all the signs of being pregnant, and I began to cluck around her as if she were my only daughter. Selfishly, I was hoping that she would produce only one cub, that it would be male, and that it would possess all the marvellous qualities I admired in Marquis, who went on living mostly in the harem (occasionally with us in The Pheasantry) to get to know his wives, and to be ready, in case the other two young lionesses came on heat, which they were slow to do.

Meanwhile, to my astonishment, Suki, one of my two grown tigers, had also been showing all the normal signs of pregnancy. became easily distressed and vicious by turn; she put on weight; her teats became prominent and she even produced milk. The vet was satisfied that she was about to give birth, but I was not—unless it was a virgin birth—because she had not been near a male tiger (unless she had somehow managed to deceive me, her mum, in the night hours, which was unlikely enough to be daft).

We called in another vet, and he made detailed tests. It was, as

I had thought, that rare and puzzling thing: a phantom pregnancy. But why? I wondered.

And then it dawned on me. I had been fussing around Lady too much, and Suki, who was always inclined to be highly-strung had noticed and been hurt; being a smart girl, she had also detected the reason, and had duplicated it to win back my affection for her. I was suitably ashamed for having neglected one of my 'cats' in this way, and I tried to be more understanding thereafter.

Tigers, when they grow up, play much rougher than lions, and are that much faster in their movements. For these reasons, Suki, although she was very well behaved on the whole, had to be consigned quite a lot to the 'cheetah run' in the garden, or, on collar and chain, to the running wire, whence she threatened to reduce the lawn to a dirt-track. So I took to talking to her more and more as I passed that way; and I tried to include her sometimes in walks, as well as singling her out for praise, when she deserved it, in training sessions—all without overdoing it, of course.

Suki was nearly four, two years older than Lady, so I thought it high time she mated. My other tiger, a two-year-old called Kumar, deemed it an excellent scheme, and in due course they produced a fine litter. Astonishingly, I was able to take the cubs from Suki—so good a mother was she— and return them without trouble. This is so unusual as to be almost miraculous. Maternity took Suki out of filming for a bit, but Kumar carried on nobly. He was excellent in front of the cameras, and had starred with Marquis in *Crooks and Coronets*.

Anticipation is important in the animal-training business. My animals have appeared in virtually all the *most* important T.V. commercials in their time; so when the Esso 'tiger in your tank' petrol idea got going, I was more than ready with my strong, beautiful and intelligent Kumar, for anything that might be wanted of us. He was trained to perfection and on his toes to go anywhere at the drop of a contract. I thought if we did a really good one, as Kumar could, news of it would go round the world.

But the expected telephone call never came and, as far as I know, they never once used a live tiger in the long advertising campaigns, either here or in the many overseas countries in which they ran.

Incidentally, Roger is rather more of a tiger man than a lioniser and, in turn, tigers seem to favour him, too. Recently we had introduced into 'the orphanage' a new Bengal tiger cub called Indira (we'd just been on a trip to India and had been somewhat impressed by the feline qualities of Mrs. Ghandi).

Indira was a special favourite with Roger, and, being a female, she took him to her heart as well. During the day she would sit at his feet in the office, ready to retreat backwards if anyone suspicious arrived on the scene, and was mainly quite content to let the others chase around the house, preferring to wait and have the occasional game with Roger.

However, on the occasion when Roger was very busy and Indira was ready for play, she would get up to all sorts of antics to attract his attention. She would waddle around his feet making S-bends with her body and miaowing loudly; and, if he continued to ignore her after a considerable time, she would scheme up some other way to 'get her man'. One was that she would go up the old back staircase which runs between the office and the kitchen and once on the top step, would create the most awful row, which would mean that Roger could neither hear on the phone nor think. So, up he would have to get, and go and rescue her, bring her back to the office, and give her a good talking to. Indira obviously thought that even a telling off from him was better than being ignored, and would snuggle into Roger, who then felt obliged to let her sit amongst his papers on the desk.

Indira is a very sturdy little tiger, with solid, almost square legs, reminiscent of an old four-poster bed. People say Bengal tigers are on the brink of extinction. While we do not believe this, there would seem to be some truth in the report that, whereas as recently as 1930, there were estimated to be forty thousand Bengal tigers in the Indian sub-continent, today, there are not more than two thousand.

As usual, man, with his gun and with his concrete-mixer, is the villain. We are doing what little we can to build up the numbers of good examples of the species, and Indira looks like being an outstandingly attractive one.

It occurs to me that I keep going into detail about the animals but *not* about my husband, so maybe this brief account will serve to give him some flesh and personality.

Between the years 1957 and 1965, a somewhat studious young man, Roger Cawley, worked for Bertram Mills Circus, rising to the exalted position of manager. Born into the most conservative and unlikely-to-change of families, at Freshwater, Isle of Wight with a splendidly staid bank-manager for a father, Roger was inevitably steered into banking in his late teens. But, secretly an incurable romantic, he had already lost his heart to the circus, while still at school, and was doomed; for all such, the only way to work some sort of salvation is for them to give what they have to the poor, and take to the road with the other unworldly souls who dedicate their lives to animals and to the public.

Roger must have known this instinctively, for he 'joined up' with circuses in his holidays, for a year or two, and then threw up his banking job altogether, as soon as he felt he could eventually be accepted by circus folk as one of them.

I first met Roger just after we had established our original zoo at Southampton. The Bertram Mills complex had set up shop a couple of hundred yards away on the common. We went to their circus and they came to our zoo. It was cosy. Roger booked some of our animals to put in the Mills's London Olympia Menagerie at Christmas. He had to negotiate mainly with me. There were vibrations.

When the time came, I took the animals to London and had to keep checking on them through the run of the show. The friendship with Roger developed pleasantly but slowly. I had other suitors and was in no hurry to make my mind up. This was in the 1963–4 winter season.

But life seldom allows us to control the pace of the events that affect our destinies. Within a year, the tents of the touring show of the Bertram Mills business had been folded and it had been bought by financier Maxwell Joseph, and he had decided to put on only one more show at Olympia. There was a big sale of animals, props and equipment in March 1964. Only three or four staff had been kept on, including Roger, to sell off the assets, and young Cawley was then out of a job until December, when he would be required to act as a manager at Olympia for the season.

I heard about all this when I was in India, accompanied by 'coals from Newcastle' in the form of a leopard, a Bengal tiger and a cheetah, all from England, who were taking part in a film called *Maya*.

The star of *Maya* was an extremely good-looking young giant, Clint Walker, with whom I had a mild flirtation, as much out of boredom as anything else. There's always a lot of hanging about when filming, and this one was particularly exasperating for various reasons, which I do not propose to go into.

Anyway, I had taken one of my cheetahs to India, a very experienced one, Teddy, who had been in *The Moonspinners* with Hayley Mills—a delightful film; and I must digress for a few lines to say that all went well on *The Moonspinners* set until one of the many technicians, then needed before a film could get under way, knocked over a boom and frightened Teddy, who promptly leaped across the studio and landed plumb in the lap of another seated technician who was reading a newspaper. My leap across the floor was just as agile and even faster than that of the cheetah, and I rescued Teddy before any harm could be done. It was always a worry in those days, the number of apparent 'spare files' the unions insisted on having in a studio during filming. It always made it harder to keep the undivided attention of my animals.

In *Maya*, I was using Teddy in a sequence in which the cheetah had to bound along the banks of a river, while a stunt man swam in the fast-flowing water, impersonating the hero. Unfortunately, Teddy, who was a bit of a fool, really, mistimed a cue and fell in the water. I'm not that much of a swimmer that I can tackle a rushing current of this power, so there I was running along the bank shouting instructions to the stunt-man to rescue my cheetah. Of course, he wasn't daft, either, and he rapidly climbed out on the opposite bank. Teddy was, in fact, less perturbed than anyone. After allowing himself to be carried downstream to a suitable bend in the river, with me in hot pursuit, he calmly swam ashore, and was shaking himself dry when I arrived at his side, quaking at what my father would say if this seven hundred and fifty pound investment was hurt in any way.

In another scene, the cheetah had to be filmed running across a road. The only way I could arrange this was to let him have a smell of his favourite food, liver, and then show him that if he ran across the road I would give him some. Unfortunately, in the process, I had got liver blood round my fingers, and, when he had finished his snack, Teddy snapped at my hand, and got my thumb before I could withdraw. Thinking it was meat, he pulled and pulled. It was hell and I shouted for help, but everyone was petrified and nobody moved. In the end I had to tap him really hard on the nose to get my hand free. It was touch and go, but my thumb was saved on this occasion. (As I have already described in my previous book, a lion not only bit the top off one of my fingers later on, but also ate it with relish!)

Teddy was unexpectedly a headache in other ways in India. For idiotic reasons of economy, the film company had only bought a minimum amount of chicken wire for caging the working areas; the netting did not quite reach, and on a running shot Teddy squeezed through a gap, with the result that we all had to chase him for several hours before we could get him back to work.

In another sequence in the same film my pet tiger, Suki, had to climb a tree and jump into a lake after the hero, Clint Walker. After we had tried the stunt out for the first time, an unexpected snag arose. Suki loved the warm water of the lake so much that, having jumped in out of the tree, she disregarded my calls and signals, preferring to splash about and have a swim. So disobedient was she that this time (the water not being fast-flowing, thank God) I had to strip off, dive in and steer her to the shore, to the sarcastic applause of the cynical film crew.

Subsequently, when we were shooting the same sequence, Suki spotted a gap in some rocks by the lake. If she had got into the middle of the dark rocks, I might never have seen her again. So, without considering the danger, I leapt forward and grabbed her tail (the only remaining visible part of her). I was obviously hurting the tiger, but I held on grimly for five minutes, in constant peril of her turning round and biting me, while someone ran to fetch my father. It was a near thing, but you never think, at the time, that these are man- (and woman-) killers you are handling, only that they are valuable and must not be lost.

I was extremely sorry to get the news about Roger, in the shape of a long letter from my mother, while I was in the midst of some fairly trying routines with my animals on the film-set near Mysore. But there's no room for sentiment these days. A very large circus had had to fold up, after several decades. To me, this was a sad event in human and animal terms rather than in the sense that it was a black day in the history of our business. Mainly, I felt desperately sorry for Roger—who had given up a safe job only seven years before—and I wanted to comfort him in the way I would comfort any stray that had been hurt. But I was too far away, and far too busy.

When filming ended on *Maya*, I had a characteristic cable from father (who had gone home ahead) asking me (*telling*, I really mean) to send my cats home by air and go at once from Mysore to Calcutta to buy animals for one of his projects. I duly did my stuff and was ready to accompany my purchases home on the ship when the bombshell fell. It came in the shape of a sharp missive from the shipping company, to the effect that they were cancelling my ticket. They had not realised, said the letter, that I was a good-looking young single girl. The ship was a cargo one, and my presence could have a catastrophic effect on the morale of the spartan, all-male members of the crew!

To say I was set back on my heels, when I read this archaic nonsense, is like saying a giraffe is taller than a dachshund.

This was in the mid-sixties, remember, with women's lib coming up fast and most of the rest of the world's merchant fleets employing women (*single* women) as crews. But Queen Victoria was not dead as far as the Indian branch of this particular shipping line was concerned. I tried every trick, but I could not shift them.

I was really in a fix. Father was tied up elsewhere; John, my younger brother was too young; my sister Margaret was at school, so she could not chaperone me (even if that might have been an acceptable arrangement on the ship, which I doubt); and brother Richard was catching game in Africa. So it looked very much like an impasse.

Then I thought of Roger Cawley, my unemployed friend. A few minutes on the telephone and I had persuaded him to pack a toothbrush and catch the next plane to Calcutta. I'd like to say we fell into each other's arms, and spent a few blissful weeks mooning around, gazing into each other's eyes. Is life ever like that for anyone, outside the films? Certainly it is not for Jimmy Chipperfield's offspring. With Roger to be paid, father decided that more animals should be shipped. So we dashed around the various dealers in the area, and rounded up what we could, including a big cow elephant which was due to calf four months later.

The elephant was a brilliant stroke, we thought. I had never known an elephant produce young in England. She would have her calf in Southampton Zoo, and great would be the resultant publicity for the Chipperfields and their enterprises.

But the best-laid schemes of elephants and men gang oft agley. After I had seen Roger and the animals safely aboard the steamer, I flew home to look after my many animal problems at Southampton. And meanwhile, Roger was having a very rough sea trip indeed, poor soul. So were the animals. And Roger, although he was a 'natural' to the business, had been mainly an administrator, and had not had the experience we had had of actually looking after animals in all possible conditions, including sea sickness. Several miscellaneous beasts were lost, alas, during the voyage, and, worst of all, the cow elephant aborted in a storm.

It was disappointing, but we could not blame Roger. We had asked a lot of him at short notice, and he had coped very well, considering. After all, he had been pretty sea-sick, himself, most of the way.

In fact, when he finally showed up at the zoo, thinner than ever he had been and more than a trifle pale, I felt so sorry for him— already 'orphaned' from the circus he loved, and thrown in at the deep end by us before he knew much more than a doggy-paddle— that, in a weak moment, I actually allowed him to propose and to fix a date in October, for our wedding. He had taken a fill-in job at a Cardiff theatre for three months, and was due at Olympia for the last time, in December.

The wedding was on a Sunday, 10 October, 1965, and took

Second birthday portrait of Marquis

Mary with Liza (*left*)
and Marquis (*below*)

place at St Michael and All Angels Church, Basset, Southampton. I was twenty-six and Roger was twenty-nine. I wore a princess-line gown of Notttingham lace with a demurely-scalloped neck line, three-quarter length sleeves and double-frilled cuffs, plus a tiara and full-length veil. The train was a very long one, also finished in Nottingham lace, and my sister Margaret and two friends (Elizabeth Dalton and Beverley Ross) were the brides-maids. They were dressed in blue silk dresses with threaded ribbons, with bouquets of roses and stephanotis. I carried red roses. Roger's brother, Graham, was best man, but apart from the Cawleys, the church was packed mainly with circus people and journalists, plus a light scattering of my boy-friend 'ex-es' from farms and stately homes, showing good humour and good will in defeat!

There was, of course, a crisis during the actual hitching ceremony, which was conducted by the rector, the Rev. F. H. Shall. A few days before the wedding, I had been unloading some pythons father had air-freighted home, and, although I have been handling them since I was a child, and have trained quite a few in my time, one of them managed to bite me. This would not have bothered me unduly, except that it chose to leave some of its thousands of teeth in the third finger of my left hand, so that it was a fearful struggle at the altar to get the ring on at all, to the consternation of some and the amusement of others.

Anyway, after I had posed for pictures in my wedding dress, with various animals, including a tiger and a rhino (it being before Marquis's birth, of course)—and after we had cut the cake—a three-tier affair surmounted by a white circus horse—we went off on honeymoon in a carriage pulled by a fine pair of greys, and for one of the few times in my life I had a good cry.

We were headed for Gibraltar, Tangiers and Casablanca, and strange looks we got from hotel desk-clerks and others at all three places; my finger had swollen so much that I had had to

E

leave my wedding ring with my mother, so that there we were on honeymoon with no visible evidence that we were married.

That's not all. Even on my honeymoon, father's shadow was present. He had briefed me well before I went off that my visit to the Middle East was an excellent opportunity to buy a few camels! So off we traipsed, Roger and I, to Marrakesh, Morocco, and there we squatted, in the smellier corners of the market, bargaining towards a deal that would ensure that we should have unpleasant company on the way home, for camels are notorious for having bad breath, as well as other notorious best-friends-won't-tell-them weaknesses. In the event, we could not get an export licence, so all the deals fell through, but it was a near thing.

When we got home, Roger had other surprises waiting for him that would keep his feet firmly on the ground. Max, my possessive one-year-old chimpanzee, had missed me so much that he had to sleep in our bed for a few nights to get over his neurosis, and Roger had to be careful when he turned over or Max would have a go at him. That's the sort of thing men who have the temerity to marry into the Chipperfield family have to put up with. But we must have something, damn it all, for over the years there has never been any shortage of suitors around the place.

Having mentioned Suki the tiger's jealousy, I mustn't leave out Phoenix's. In addition to my lions, tigers, cheetah and leopard, among my personal 'wild cats' at The Pheasantry, is a black panther, Phoenix, who looks rather like an over-grown domestic cat, with brilliant green eyes and quite a small head for his rather large body. He is, however, very far from being docile, and would quickly get the better of anyone taking liberties with him.

Phoenix has his lair in the backyard, near where I groom my horses. He is extremely jealous, as the green eyes would suggest, and would never begin to allow me to neglect him for another, as Suki had done. If I am busy with the horses, and ignoring him, for just a moment, he paces up and down swishing his long tail and making the most weird eeee-ing noise. To pacify him, I have to chat him up cheerfully, tell him he's loved, and tickle his nose, whereupon he quietens down a bit; but no one else is allowed the privilege of putting a finger near him. I am his only mistress and he is extremely ferocious towards the rest of the world. So, although we have anything up to ten large canines around the place at any given day, far and away the finest guard-dog at The Pheasantry is Phoenix, the black panther.

On a grassy bank by the stables, very close by Phoenix's quarters, we've had a friendly covey of partridges, more or less in residence, for most of the winter. They cannot know whence comes the panther, or his alleged ferociousness, nor do they fear him in any way, but it is a fascinating study to see how the game family instinctively and carefully obeys the international rules of the prey war.

These are that if the 'enemy' (in this case Phoenix) approaches slowly, the birds withdraw equally slowly, carrying on with what they are doing, moving only as the situation demands and only far enough to preserve the all-important flight distance, which is known with absolute accuracy to the weak of all species by instinct, as the safe interval if escape is demanded. If, however, the enemy moves suddenly, then flight reaction is triggered instantly, after which the potential prey will take some time to settle again.

But, as I mentioned earlier, any birds big enough to interest a wild animal notice instantly a well-filled belly and mainly relax in such circumstances, within the exigencies of the broader aspects of the prey war rules.

So the plump female dumplings pecked away in the grass, while father partridge vainly preened his earth-coloured feathers near by, and the only times I ever heard warning squawks out of him were (1) when Charles, the chimp, hove-to one day (when

Phoenix was absent from his lair, of course, or he would not have dared approach) and decided it would be fun to chase some birds — especially fat, slow-flying ones like these; and (2) when Donja, my ten-year-old Indian elephant, who had been brought over from the farm where she had been stabled, was frightened by a field mouse one day, and scared the pants off everyone in earshot with her trumpeting. Fully-grown, Donja was bought in September 1966, just after David was born. Alas, she had rather a bad disposition, generally, and was given to taking off over the fields when she was feeling perverse. We had, therefore, decided to ship her shortly to our American park.

On the other hand, Wamba, my other elephant, who was in the film *Julius Caesar*, and has a series of TV commercials going, has a sweet nature. She was caught by my brother, Richard, five years ago in the bush. She is quite bright—a natural performer who can do all the usual tricks and can beg appealingly. She is not normally frightened of other animals or of traffic.

We proposed eventually to introduce a herd of elephants to the game reserves at Longleat and elsewhere, but there were problems over this—notably the fact that, despite their great dignity, they can be a threat to their habitat, and particularly to the wooded parts of the reserve, because they tend to feed off the crowns of trees, to rip off branches, and to knock or push trees over, either intentionally or accidentally. They are sloppy feeders, and are liable to excrete noisily, in unison, to the surprise of the on-lookers, to put it mildly.

It was hard to believe that Marquis was two years old, but he was, on 6 February, 1968. His birthday was spent, as it happened, in a hot TV studio, making a carpet commercial, but he had a delicious meal of goat meat as a treat, before he left home. So big was he now, at about twenty-five stone, that it had been deemed advisable to have a stake driven into the floor through the middle of the carpet, to which he could be tethered when I was away from him. 'Why is he smacking his lips?' asked a cameraman as he zoomed in on the lion's bow-shaped but extremely large mouth. 'Because he sees his dinner flying towards him,' I answered cheerfully.

There was never a month went past without film or TV work coming up for one or several of my animals, but, as that is what justifies their semi-luxurious existence, I never complained about the early rising or the long hours involved. The one thing I tend to dread is being stuck with someone else's problems after a film (the more so as this happens to me through 'friendships' often enough in life, anyway).

A few months before this, as I recounted more fully in *Lions on the Lawn*, Father and I had supplied every animal required, when it came to the bit, for the filming of *Dr. Dolittle* at Castle Combe, even to a fox *and* the hounds to chase it ('by kind permission', as they say, of the illustrious Duke of Beaufort). But what I did not say was that the film people had had arrangements with certain American trainers, as a result of which a few animals had been brought to England from the States, including a dog, which never did a day's work, two chimps and two sea-lions.

After the filming had ended, we found ourselves looking after one of their seals, who was ill. We kept him in the bath (and washed at the basin ourselves) for a couple of weeks while the vet treated him. It was awful. He was a nice quiet fellow, who was never happier than when he was giving you a kiss, or balancing the sponge on his nose, or slapping with his flippers; but first the bathroom, and then the whole of The Pheasantry, came to stink of sick and of fish. He recovered eventually, thank goodness, and was shipped back to the States in a wet tank.

The two Jersey cows which shake a leg in the film were brought in (as almost the only performing animals we did not already possess). I became so fond of one of them that she was found a shed at the bottom of the orchard at The Pheasantry and is still there, which is why milking was added to my many morning and evening chores, on any days we were really short of help! The first few weeks were the funniest (hilarious, in fact) because I was heavily pregnant then and could only just reach Lulu-Belle's teats with my arms fully stretched.

There was also a young Poll Hereford Bull, with a very beautiful face and figure, who was scheduled to appear in the film, but in the end, alas, was written out. We had him in the stables for a bit, but felt this was unfair, as Lulu-Belle was not his type, and there were neither cows around for his pleasure nor work in prospect to fulfil him. So he was sent off to earn his cattle-cake serving a herd in Worcestershire.

I never like buying-in animals just for one film. As I said before, you've got to live with animals to understand them and get the best performances out of them. But the Disney people have been so good to me over the years (giving my animals a monopoly of all Disney films made in Europe since I began in animal training as a teenager a dozen or more years ago) that I would truly do anything for them.

In one particular Disney film, *The Horse Without A Head*, in which I had fifty dogs performing in one way or another, it just happened that I did not have a pooch with the correct vocal chords for a concluding sound sequence, in which a dog would be heard in a rage, growling, barking and roaring. I managed to get hold of a mongrel dog who was perfect in the part, but soon found he had a fierce and unpredictable temper. In the early stages of training I discovered that he would snap at me if I was getting the best results out of him. I went ahead, anyway, taking the calculated risk that, if I wore gloves, he would not do much damage.

In the event, while they were recording his frenzied voice, he was going for my hands with greater ferocity than ever. Before long, it got so bad they had to stop (muggins me! I would have continued until they had all they wanted, as I did not want to spoil a good 'take') and rush me to the studio doctor, who had to stitch up both my hands, so severely had the mongrel bitten through the gloves. But it's all in a day's work, if you take your job seriously.

I get upset more by the men around film studios who faint at the sight of blood, or who take the opposite line—that only men are tough, and women *must* be the weaker sex—to the point that they will try to interfere with my work.

A perfect example of this was another Disney film, *The Horse-masters*, around which there were more layabouts, claiming to be horse experts, than there were bags of oats for the real stars of the film.

I have a marvellous chestnut stallion, High Endeavour, spirited, lively and handsome, who would obey no one but me from the day I got him. Not even leading show-jumpers of the day, used to breaking young horses, had been able to do anything with him.

In one sequence in *The Horsemasters*, High Endeavour (who was named after the title of a book, written by circus artist Edward Seago, about my father's wartime career as an R.A.F. fighter pilot) was required to knock over a girl and gallop off into the middle distance as if the clappers of hell were ringing in his ears.

Every time we did this sequence (and there were many takes) I got fairly heavily bruised, because I stood in for Millicent Martin as the girl the horse knocked over, and High Endeavour quite rightly played his part for real, not wanting to hurt me, but not holding back, either.

Anyway, as I say, because it was a horse picture, there were all these clever jerks around, who could, so they said, ride or round-up anything on legs. They would come over to pick me up after the spill, and would boringly, parrot-wise, all say the same sort of thing, like, 'Say, missee, don't you worry about that little old horse o' yourn today; I'll have it back for you in two shakes of a mare's ass.'

I got weary of trying to argue. So it was that, each day, one big, tough horseman would ride off into the blue to bring back High Endeavour. And so it was that each day, some hours later, one big, tough horseman would return, tired, deflated and empty-handed, and I would have to go out into the gathering dusk to bring back my horse myself, as usual.

The only other person who just about made it with High Endeavour was Alan Oliver, who subsequently made money show-jumping some of our other horses for us; but even he had difficulties.

The best stunt-rider in the film business tried out the stallion and had the skin worn off his legs to the point that they were raw for days.

High Endeavour is the strongest horse I have ever known. To get him in anything like a restrained-enough condition to be worked in a film, I always had to gallop him like mad for an hour. Even after this, he would be full of it, and would still jog-trot to the location, trying to throw his head around in rebellion.

Occasionally, he even tried it on with me and suddenly moved to run off and unseat me. But I was as wily as he was. As soon as I saw what he was up to, I took a foot out of one stirrup and dropped the reins. Thinking I was getting off, and not wishing to hurt me, he stopped instantly. In some ways he was just a big daft beggar, meaning no harm, but he was also so powerful, his high spirits were exhausting.

The Horsemasters, being made mainly at Shepperton Studios, was, in fact, the first of more than a dozen Disney pictures we took part in in very quick succession. I was seventeen at the time; it was my first real experience of filming; and I was utterly determined to succeed. Although I knew nothing about films, I knew a very great deal about horses.

I got the job because others had tried to follow the script's difficult requirement for various manœuvres involving 'a wild stallion,' and had failed.

High Endeavour was a stallion all right and he certainly was 'wild'. All my horses are, in fact, stallions, for reasons of temperament, and for breeding purposes. High Endeavour was, in truth, the very first horse to be all my own. His spirit and courage were such that I made a lot of money with him in the show-jumping ring.

I now have upwards of a dozen horses around the place at any given time, mainly because I love riding them, but partly because (a) I can't resist acquiring them, and (b) because they are always trained and ready for film work.

In The Horsemasters, I had to work High Endeavour many times completely out in the open, for the dramatic sequences, which is a very much more difficult matter than working an animal indoors. Perhaps the hardest trick was when he had to rear up and send the villain for six, but he got it right first time. Galloping off into the country on his own, after knocking over the girl, was the next most challenging aspect of his part in the film, but we got that right, too. Thereafter, Disney not only used us all the time, but, before he died, he gave me a medal recording the pleasure it had been to work with me in every film made outside America.

As I have said, Marquis behaves impeccably, under the most trying circumstances, before the cameras, but certain things worry him unpredictably. An example was the James Bond film, Casino Royale in which he had to jump on to a Rolls Royce. Normally he would land from a jump with his claws sheathed, but something about the elegant car (probably its mirrored paintwork) upset him to the point that he scratched it heavily every time he landed, and it had to be taken away for a respray after every 'take'.

Speaking of films, I learned at this time, to my amusement, that Lord Bath had introduced a touch of the Metro-Goldwyn-Mayers to the proceedings at Longleat, by having a Marquis-style lion's head on his cheques, like an embossed stamp-duty emblem. The Marquess devised the design himself, feeling that a personalised symbol (in addition to his coat of arms—motto: 'I have a good cause') could do no harm. The bank—the Westminster, at Warminster—is also uniquely honoured in that it alone has an account listed solely as 'lions'. That's show business!

In a similar vein, we had devised window-stickers for cars, and one was included in the admission pack given to each motorist visitor. Around a head of Marquis was the legend 'We have seen the Lions of Longleat'. Reports subsequently filtered in to say that these stickers had been spotted on cars in all parts of Europe and even in America. But the most amusing backlash (if you can call it that) was confided to us by one of the coach-drivers who regularly visited us with parties of tourists. 'You've got old Bedford rattled, miss,' he told me. ''E won't let any coach into Woburn if it carries a Longleat sticker!'

This was certainly one up to us in the Stately Home Stakes, for the Duke of Bedford had previously been the most successful of all the house-openers, but moves were afoot that would radically change the old rivalries between several of the top-of-the-pops estates.

The truth was, although we would have bitten our tongues off rather than have revealed a word of it, our father, which art everywhere at once, or so you might think, had been having talks with two leading English aristocrats, including Bedford, astonishingly (and one titled landed-gentleman in Scotland), about doing Longleat-style deals with them—this while he was preparing to open reserves in all the Common Market countries, in Ireland, in Australia and in Canada. *High Endeavour* had certainly been the right title for the book about father (as well as for my horse).

Once either of them gets a bit between his teeth, there are few alive who can stop them.

Mother is a totally different animal from father—easy-going and happy-go-lucky, not to say scatter-brained at times—which is just as it should be. Her maiden name was Rosie Purchase, and she, too, is descended from a long line of circus animal-trainers. While father is away (which is most of the time) she keeps a friendly eye on things at our Zoo and Quarantine Station at Southampton.

Mother danced in lions' cages when she was young, and had the terrible experience of seeing her father, Captain Purchase, killed by his lions; he had a peg leg, over which he had tripped one day and a lion had seized the opportunity to prove that no wild beast can ever be trusted; it bit him through the spine, and, although my uncle Dick Chipperfield bravely got him out of the cage, the good Captain died in hospital soon afterwards. This was before I was born.

The Fossetts, another leading circus family, are also our relatives through marriage, my aunt Maude (one of father's sisters) having married Tom Fossett, with whom she established a very good trapeze and juggling act.

Mother's mother did a rope-spinning act and my father's mother's father (my great-grandfather) was one of the best-known horse trainers of his day, George Seaton by name. One of my great-great-grandfathers, in order to draw the crowds, used to balance a cartwheel on his chin outside the tent, and, as a change would sometimes carry a donkey up a ladder. And one of my grandfathers was a clown of international repute, as well as having other circus skills, versatility being one of the eternal disciplines necessary in families such as ours. In his case, he was also adept at carving and painting circus wagons as well as playing various instruments in the band. It is all part of three hundred years and more of such traditions on both sides of the family, of which I am rightly proud.

Mother is quite incorrigible, in the nicest way. There was the time when she bought a considerable quantity of national insurance stamps to put on the staff's cards at Southampton. Somehow, on the way home, they got very wet. So she put them in a pan and tried to dry them out on the cooker. Instead, of course, they went all messy, stuck together and curled up into an almost unrecognisable bundle, as well as sticking to the metal. So she marched back to the post-office, with the pan of stamp stew, and cheerfully demanded replacements. The post-office people got very shirty about it, but mother never worries. She left it with them to sort out at their leisure.

A few weeks later, she happened to be in the same post-office, when a different woman, a proper chatterbox, was serving; and this gossip at once proceeded to tell the tale at length, and in some awe, about the crazy woman who had brought in the national insurance stamps still steaming. The counter-hand had obviously been recounting it daily ever since to every customer. Mother allowed her to finish and then said chirpily. 'I know, my dear. It was me! Got my replacement stamps yet?'

Not content with this, a few months later mother happened to be doing the stamps again; this time she forgot she had them in a suit pocket and sent it to be dry-cleaned. The stamps looked a bit odd when she got the suit back and fished them out, but she stuck them on the cards nevertheless. In due course, a letter arrived asking why 'faded' stamps had been used. 'It was probably the bleach that did it,' mother wrote back, without amplification. They're probably still trying to figure that one out.

Another day, she had just come out of hair-stylist Raymonde's Southampton branch (all glammed up and wearing her finest 'duchess' clothes and jewels) when one of the 'hands' from the zoo zoomed up on a smelly old motor-cycle. Seeing mother, and knowing what a softy she is, he handed over the bike with the injunction: 'Just keep the engine running while I buy some fags,

Mrs. C. If it stops, it's the very devil to get going again.' So mother stood there doing as requested. Meanwhile, a queue was forming at an adjoining bus stop, and, of course, they began to scratch their thatch and talk amongst themselves in complete puzzlement at the sight of a magnificently coiffed and groomed lady revving like mad on the hand throttle of an ancient and filthy racing-motor-cycle. Fortunately, the bus arrived and took them away, or they might have been even more alarmed to hear mother's language, shouted towards the cigarette kiosk, when her Rolls-Royce arrived, and the lad had not emerged to take over his bike!

You may have seen mother, by the way, when we all trooped in to greet father, James Seaton Methuen Chipperfield, when he was the subject of *This Is Your Life* on television a few years ago. They ought to do *her* some time and you'd hear some stories, I can tell you!

5

More to see than in Africa

THE ROAD from the lion-crested entrance gates at Longleat descends first into a small valley, then curls up a low hill, continuing to the crown, before veering abruptly left into a slow descent. A sharp right turn and a climb then bring you to the edge of a fairly steep hillock, with a small meadow and a rivulet below, leading to the double-doored exit. All the way there are lions and cubs to be observed, enjoying family life in the pride as much as any family from anywhere in any car.

The reserve is mostly woodland, but not so thick you cannot see the lions for the trees. As *Personality*, a South African magazine put it: 'After all, not even our most famous game reserve, the Kruger Park, can guarantee you numbers of lions, like Longleat does, on a single visit.'

Visitors have several times put this to me in a different, and flattering, way. What they generally say is that they had previously spent hundred of pounds and travelled thousands of miles on safari tours to Africa and had returned after weeks, having scarcely seen one ropey old lion. Yet in a single day they had seen up to fifty of the royal beasts, in prime condition, for a pound in Wiltshire, within easy motoring distance of their homes.

Successful breeding was now going on apace in the reserve, to the point that triangular warning signs had had to be erected at lion-crossing points (the idea of *zebra* crossings have been rejected regretfully as too silly for a serious reserve) bearing the message 'SLOW. Beware of lion cubs on the road.' Sneaky, one of our most affectionate lionesses, was rearing two of her own at this stage, plus another two she had adopted, and they were wont to play rather near the road. All the cubs had been fathered by Nigel, a splendid specimen, who—like most men—left the chores of bringing up the babies to his spouse, while he gruffly courted a younger lioness.

We now had a fantastic variety of lions in the park, including some with skins of pale chestnut and manes of dark chestnut shading to dark brown and almost black; the manes in these cases run under the body, right across the belly, almost to the back legs—thick matted manes, like tattered fleeces. These particular lions also have comically blunt snub-noses, rather like those in ancient Egyptian wall drawings. In general, the colours of the 'Kings' of the reserve range from darkish brown, through gingery red and marmalade, to underdone-biscuit; their coats vary from thick-matted fur to fine-silk hair; their manes range the scale from the full bit to mere collars. In our efforts towards a breeding-strain that would be healthy, intelligent and attractive, we called in various advisers, including Professor F. B. Hunt of Cornell University, a world expert on genetic breeding problems. He had also made a special study of white rhinos, and my father made a point of having long talks with him on this subject—with very good reason, for we already had several of these stupendous beasts in quarantine.

Around the winding road that snakes through the reserve, we meanwhile tried to keep all our notices fresh, and changed the

wording, for maximum impact, from time to time. That famili-
arity truly breeds contempt there can be no denying, *viz* the
cynical but partly true notice I saw in a golf club on the outskirts
of Nairobi: 'A ball lying less than ten yards from a lion need not
be played until later.' But it is necessary to be watchful at all times
with wild animals, no matter how familiar they may be to you,
and that was the principle we followed daily at Longleat.

A gentleman from Yorkshire bowled into the reserve one day late
in February, driving a glass-fibre-bodied Lotus sports car. He had
two girl passengers and soon they all stopped for a smoke, part
opening the side window screens for the purpose. Almost at once,
Atlas, the largest lion in the park, appeared and snatched at the
screen on the driver's side. One swipe dislodged it, but it fell into
the car. So the wise and amiable lion went round to the other side,
grabbed at the other screen and made off with it into the woods.
The man concerned, who made light of the event, told us later
that he had been a game warden in Bechuanaland for years and
had never once seen a lion. We paid for a new side window and
had to decide that cars of this type could not be admitted in
future. If anyone turned up in one, they were asked to park it
and were treated to a run round the reserve in one of the Safari
Mini-buses (Ford Transit Combos, in zebra livery) we use for
the conveyance of car-less visitors.

I had to waste part of the same day, as could happen when our
PRO was absent, taking a Kenyan reporter—a female, in
winter woolies—around the estate. But bless her, she subsequently reported sincerely—on the sort of lines we were now
becoming accustomed to—that she had seen more lions at Longleat in half-an-hour, and all first-class specimens, than she had
seen in a three-day safari at home.

Another day about this time, a box of matches caught fire in a
visitor's jacket. He was in a terrible predicament, not knowing
whether to leap out into the middle of a pride and be eaten or

'What do you mean – no bananas today?'

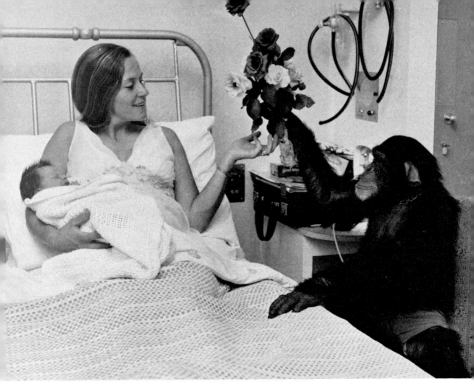

Charles visiting Mary in Salisbury Infirmary when Suzanne was born

At The Pheasantry the baby must be caged rather than the animals

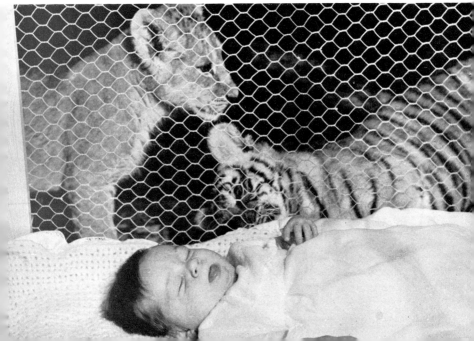

remain in the driving seat and roast to death. In the end, he wisely blew his horn, while beating at the flames, and a warden was with him in a twinkle, so that he did not suffer too much.

Even this early in the year, there was a continuance of minor problems within the reserve, as when two anti-German lions, playing with a bone, bounced into the side of a Mercedes and did coachwork damage which cost us thirty pounds. But in the main there was no trouble, and cartoonists took up the inverted idea that most of the lions thought it cruel, the way humans were kept cooped up in cars all the time. And an Australian journalist wrote home to say that the 'speed track' road from Warminster to Frome was much more dangerous than the road around the lion park.

Meanwhile our few home-owner-neighbours, not connected with the Bath estate, who had found themselves (in the early days of the project) questioned by the Press and by local officials about their attitude to having lions in their midst, had had nearly two years of comparative peace. They had also lost, for ever we hoped, their early fears or conjectures that lions might escape one night to pillage their rose gardens and to devour their pekes—or worse!

Work was by now well advanced on a picnic area and an East African Game Park, adjoining the lion reserve. These were due to open within a few weeks, barring weather hold-ups or other unforeseen circumstances.

A new five-hundred-seater restaurant was being built (with nude sixty-foot murals to be added by Lord Bath's heir, thirty-four-year-old Viscount Weymouth, depicting Heaven and Hell) in connection with this project, and the labourers were working on it long hours so that it could be ready for the start of the season proper, at Easter, whether the new reserve opened with it or not.

As they sat wearily round a brazier, having a deserved breather and brewing-up, one morning, I happened that way with Marquis. No one moved as my lion got nearer and nearer, but I could almost

F

hear the bristles rising in fear on the backs of the men's necks at the sight of a three-and-a-half hundredweight 'man-eater' approaching their tea-party. Before we were too close I bade Marquis 'sit' and he did so immediately. Seeing how obedient he was, the men became more relaxed and offered me a mug of tea, which I accepted. Then an Irish labourer made so bold as to approach Marquis with an enamel mug of the steaming hot brew. I had no idea how my friend would react to this, so I remained watchful, and waited. As the mug was placed before him, however, the steam got up Marquis's huge nostrils, and he opened his jaws wide in puzzlement, just as the Paddy was affecting a curtsey before the 'King'. The sight of the cavernous open mouth suddenly appearing inches in front of him was such a shock to the man that he was off, quicker than you could say 'what's new, pussycat', and must have broken the record for the mile (and over obstacles at that) before he stopped.

Meanwhile, I was explaining to the others that they had nothing to fear but fear itself (or words to that effect) and to prove it, I placed a contractor's tin hat, that was lying near by, on Marquis's huge head and gave him a cuddle. We subsequently took a picture of Marquis in his steel safety helmet, with a pot of tea between his paws, and it was a riot—published by newspapers and magazines all over the world. As so often happens, a natural situation had naturally become a publicity stunt, if you care to call it that.

Occasionally journalists would wish to interview the Marquess of Bath in the company of a lion, so Marquis, who was most suitable for the job as well as most dramatic, was soon no stranger to the Titians and tapestries; the lacquer and the lackeys; the Chippendale furniture and Chelsea porcelain; the family portraits, by van Dyck, Reynolds, Lely, Lawrence, Orpen, Topolski; and the copy-Rubens, in the entrance hall, entitled *Lion Hunt* and showing white hunters being bloodily savaged by some of his huge ancestors in Africa. The Bath coat of arms also may not have escaped his attention, featuring as it does lions rampant with knotted tails (which had something to do with the taming of the Scots).

Marquis also got on extremely well with the Marquess's Rhodesian Ridgeback dog—appropriately named Leo.

Drinks are usually served in the long library, which serves many functions these days—as well as housing one of the finest private book-collections in the western world, some thirty thousand volumes, tentatively valued at two million pounds.

In our family (the Chipperfields, that is) we neither smoke nor drink—partly because our health and fitness are what keep us at the peak in our peculiar line of business. But we're not silly about it, and when Booth's Gin chose Marquis as 'the greatest lion in the world' early in 1968, we took it as as big a compliment as if it had been conferred by Scotts' porridge oats, or the Kennel Club, or what have you.

As well as having many pictures taken, as the celebrated King of Gin, Marquis was asked to attend a special ceremony at Longleat as Star of the Stars—those lower down the bill including Pete Murray, Richard Murdoch, Jackie Rae, Sheila Scott, Ben Warriss, Macdonald Hobley, Peter Haigh and Christopher Lee. The occasion was the presentation of a fabulous hand-made leather collar, studded in silver, to the 'King'. This was placed round Marquis's huge neck by a somewhat nervous Tommy Trinder, while I stood by explaining to the lion that everything was all right; while a brewery chief circled overhead in a helicopter; while Sheila Scott was unnecessarily assuring Tommy that flying round the world was a much easier and safer gambit; and while Christopher Lee was extolling the virtues of vampires as friendly creatures compared to lions.

Actually, I have to say that old Marquis behaved regally, and that he is very fond of the huge Booth's collar, which he is only allowed on very special occasions, as when he goes to church on a Sunday.

The same week-end, more seriously, in the interests of science, a new device was tried out on Marquis. This was a clinical thermometer, incorporating an infra-red section. Invented by experts at Mullard's, it was particularly appealing to us in that it did not have to be put in an animal's mouth. It works just as well by picking up infra-red body heat and instantly registering body temperature therefrom. Developed from military devices which can 'see' troops at night, it seemed to me to be a most excellent idea for veterinary use.

I noted, with wry amusement, in the dozens of tests that were carried out on him, that Marquis's temperature was perfectly normal. A few short weeks before, it might have been different. But the two other lionesses in his lair had still not come on heat, and Lady was about half-way through her pregnancy, so there was nothing to excite his blood at the moment.

We still went for our walks most mornings and our combined nature-study lessons around the parklands had been resumed, with spring about to burst on us at any time.

I had noticed over the three years we had been at The Pheasantry that the brown hare was returning to the fields of Wiltshire, after many years of persecution. I welcomed this trend the more as he is an ancient resident of our lands—one of our earliest mammals, with an Anglo-Saxon name, and fossilised ancestors said to be at least fifteen thousand years old.

Although the hare and the rabbit may seem to the untrained eye to be brothers, the resemblances are mainly superficial, and the animals follow very different patterns of behaviour, as well as being different in structure. Also, whereas there is only one kind of rabbit in England, there are three distinct species of hare.

The brown hares around here these days are strong, plump fellows of up to ten pounds in weight; they have very long black-tipped ears and the hind legs of a trained hurdler. All these features make them larger than and very different from any native rabbit. With their laterally-placed large brown eyes they can see all around at once and their russet coat (although brighter than a rabbit's) makes them extremely difficult to spot when they freeze and lie doggo, as they often do to protect themselves from prowling predators, of whom Mary and Marquis must both be counted examples.

One of the most positive differences is that the hare does not have an underground home. Instead of the tunnelled warrens of the bunnies, Mr. and Mrs. Hare snuggle up in hides or 'forms' in grass or bracken, whence they make their solitary and often daring forays in search of food. There is none of the gregariousness about them that rabbit colonies usually feature.

Although Marquis often raised a rabbit, mainly for the fun of it, he was less often able to follow the spoor of a hare, although we had once or twice caught glimpses of them at Castle Combe and subsequently at Longleat when we had evening walks, rather than on the more regular morning ones. Evening is the hare's usual time for expeditions to turnip, wheat or clover fields for a nibble.

We probably saw less of them because they are among the most cunning of creatures at covering up their scent when returning to their hides. As well as changing direction sharply and fre-quently, they always try to cross wet or swampy ground on the way as a sure means of throwing off nose-led pursuit. The hare is, incidentally, a strong swimmer and more than once I have seen them strike out into the long leat when frightened. By contrast, the rabbit will generally avoid water.

Probably because he has been hunted in the lowlands of England for thousands of years (and pursued for centuries by greyhounds in the sport known as coursing) the hare is a lone wolf of a creature, gregarious only in the rutting season. But he has commanded a special terminology, arising from admiration and regard, as with the horse, the fox and the stag. A hare in its first year is a leveret; in its second it is a hare; in its third it is a great hare; a male is a buck or a jack, while a female is a doe.

Although they do not 'breed like rabbits', the doe may have several litters in a year, always in the hide. Unlike any other rodent in England, baby leverets are covered with fur at birth and have full use of their eyes (as tigers do, and lions sometimes, too).

Hares are deserted from the moment they are weaned, for the very good reason that usually there will be another multiple-birth due before long. Like a lioness, a doe, once she accepts her young, will protect them with astonishing bravery every moment until they leave the 'nest'.

Shy, brown hares had fascinated Marquis since he saw his first one as a very young cub, but never once had he been able to get within striking or even sniffing distance of one. Their extreme alertness, their artful covering up of trails and their ability to run at great speed (often in eccentric circles, at that) had puzzled and baffled my lordly lion for years. Now, unknown to either of us, he was to have his great chance at last—and was to fluff it like the soppy thing he is.

Spring had begun promptly, for once, in the south-west, with violets of all colours already upstanding, and yellow crocuses, with egg on their faces, smiling at the world. We had gone out together, into this newly-created wonderland, Marquis and I, to scour the approach lanes, fields and woods for any new sights nature had to offer us. It was late March, but the snowdrops were still around to greet the newcomers, finer and taller than for some years. Not having been flattened by rain or snow in February, they had come through into March strong and clean. I poked about under the hedgerows, where they were at their best, with Marquis sniffing and snuffling amongst them, and then we followed a trail and marvelled at the numbers of these pure and lovely flowers ramping across a sheep paddock, totalling perhaps a thousand in all.

We bounded across the fresh grass together, for the sheer pleasure of it, avoiding the nodding snowdrops with our steps, and were within sight of the opposite hedgerow when suddenly Marquis stopped in his tracks, crouched down, ears back, and froze low against the turves. I had been gambolling along merrily, enjoying the spring of the new grass, and not looking ahead. Now I followed the direction of the lion's alert gaze and just could not believe my eyes. At the far side of the field, where the violets and snowdrops were thickest, and where the pink Lent roses were clustered, a congregation of hares were dancing and fighting, oblivious to our approach. There must have been fifty of them, cavorting, racing around, squatting with their paws up, pugilistic-style, leaping, pirouetting and dancing. We watched spellbound for a whole long minute. Marquis's tail was swishing slowly, and his ears remained alert, but otherwise he was as bemused as I was. Although I had heard tell often enough of the love-making antics of the mad March hare, this was the first time I had been privileged to watch the magic of the occasion.

All at once, a squeal of alarm went up, from one of the females I think (and a very young specimen at that), for all the world like the cry of a young child in pain. Several others joined in the squealing, while the older hares grunted. Led apparently by the patriarch of the group, a huge ten-pounder with ears much longer than his head, the spring-fevered group simply melted away into the woods beyond the hedge, so that by the time Marquis had caught his breath and realised that he was sitting pretty for once, and was supposed, as a beast of prey, to catch and kill these lesser creatures, the improbable play was over and there was not a hare to be seen anywhere. Growling, Marquis would have chased the trails anyway, until bamboozled once more by the damp ground beyond the trees, but I held firmly to his collar. The wind in the south-west, was bringing storm clouds across the watery white sun, so it was homewards we needs must go.

As we trotted back to The Pheasantry by a different route, I mused aloud about spring, and the effect the vernal equinox has on people as well as on animals, and my lion was reassured, at least by the tone of my voice, that what he had seen had been extraordinary and that his reaction to it had been no more than normal. *En route*, it was a pleasure to our eyes that farm and estate workers had already given vent to bursts of spring cleanliness—with verges trimmed, flower beds forked, carrots sown and onion-beds smooth as silk. The spring, that uplifting as well as maddening time, was neither forward nor backward, but just right, and the hares were in season in timely fashion, like Marquis's Lady bride in the new straw of the harem.

Like the Lord of the Bible, the Marquess of Bath likes to walk among the crowds and be mistaken perhaps for the gardener (although I must say there have been no reports to date of him walking on the water at Half-Mile Pond!) Inevitably, the 'gardener' hoax seldom works, the more so as he affects an immediately-noticeable red and white spotted handkerchief of the sort tramps once wrapped their belongings in, which nigger nannies used to use as headscarves; and more often he is caught in a large crowd of autograph seekers, which does not displease him unduly I would guess.

Over the Easter week-end in 1968, he was absolutely staggered, when he sauntered over to the main gates, to see the extent of the crowds waiting to gain admittance to the lion park, apart altogether from the throngs in other parts of the estate. There were three thousand five hundred visitors on the Saturday (and eight thousand over the week-end) so that the gates had to be kept closed much of the time and only opened at carefully-regulated intervals. Reports flowed in, from police and motoring organisations, that all approach roads were jammed and that there was a queue of cars on the main road stretching back seven miles to Bishopstowe. A new complaint came from several local riding-schools that, not only were their pupils having difficulty in getting to and from home, but also the tarmacadam was being so polished by cars that horses were falling on the country roads.

In this connection, it has been fascinating to note how the English denizens of the general locality have adjusted to the ever-increasing invasion by the car-borne public. In particular, the native hedgehog has had to change his habits. It used to be, when there were only a few of us around and he was endangered only by human feet, horses' hooves, and the very occasional vehicle, he adopted the traditional gambit his mum had taught him when he was little bigger than a pin-cushion, and rolled himself into a ball—not caring if he got kicked into the ditch or the under-growth as a result.

Then came the phase when dozens of these delightful spikey balls, which do so much good around the place by eating up grubs and insects, were being squashed by the cars they had rolled up to avoid.

But somehow the message had got round to their surviving relatives and friends, via the bush telegraph, of course, and it was now amusing, as well as a pleasure, to see that our hedgehog friends had developed a new and inspired reaction when caught in the road by the threat of the approaching car. Instead of rolling up, they had taken to running like hell for the nearest cover!

6

Nature's skyscrapers

A NEW
and very important development at Longleat reached fruition in
May, 1968. This was the extensive new East African Game Park,
which had been many months in parturition alongside the Lion
Reserve, where the estate's deer had once roamed free, and where
many species, some of them vanishing varieties, were to be established and exhibited in unhindered conditions and at no extra
charge to the paying public.

A further hundred acres of parkland had been devoted to this
project, more than doubling the area open to the public; massive
heated animal-buildings had been constructed, together with
fences, another three miles of circulatory roads, toilets, a motor
overflow park, and other amenities.

The main animal feature of the Game Park was now complete
and ready to meet its public—the largest herd of giraffes outside
Africa, spectacularly roaming the open parkland set aside for
them—and the supporting cast was to feature the giraffe's
natural associates, including a large herd of zebras, antelopes of
various sorts, Ankole cattle, ostriches, pelicans, East African

crowned cranes, and marabou storks. Endless opportunities for photography, and for the study of these animals and birds at very close range, were thereafter freely available. In addition, a huge colony of African baboons was being introduced separately, near by, so that the new attractions, together with the existing ones of lions, hippos and chimpanzees, meant that we were well advanced in our aim of presenting a comprehensive collection of African fauna in the best possible conditions and in settings that were very similar to the native ones, except for the climate, which we could not do anything about, and to which the animals and birds had quickly adapted themselves, anyway.

As more and more allegedly 'civilised' encroachments on the remaining areas of bush-land in Africa take place, the game there is being rapidly depleted, to the point that reserves can no longer be set up quickly enough to cope. Incredible though it may seem at this distance, the fact is that it can only be a matter of years before no game at all is left in the wild state. I believe that what my father has been able to do at Longleat—and in our half-dozen other parks—in terms of conservation alone, has been both timely and far-sighted. To preserve the wild life of Africa, and of other excitingly 'different' areas of the world, for future generations, it is becoming more and more important that reserves such as ours should establish ever-bigger breeding-groups, and that frequent exchanges of animals should occur, to retain and improve the best strains in each species.

In a sense, we were also reversing the trend taken by civilisation, and were giving something back to nature instead of taking it away, and we were creating opportunities (absent for centuries from animal-loving England) for the proper study or wild-animal morals, manners and conduct in the raw.

Already, by the early summer of 1968, Longleat was dramatically establishing itself as the leading centre in England for the breeding, study and conservation of Africa's wild life. To this end, we were also actively supporting the East African Wildlife Society in its efforts to preserve such game, collecting donations and selling souvenirs to help this cause.

One of the marvellous features of the new Game Park was to be that families would be allowed to leave their cars and wander around at will, even picnicking if they wished, as long as they did not attempt to touch or feed the animals, some of which are of a nervous disposition and easily frightened: indeed, it is characteristic of *all* these new animals that they are more afraid of people than people are of them: they are only ever dangerous if cornered or badly scared.

Also, the new park would undoubtedly relieve the pressures that had been building up at the lion reserve, where queues at week-ends and on public holidays had sometimes been frighteningly long. In association with the new park, a traffic-management scheme for the five miles of lion reserve and associated roads was being brought into operation.

The seventeen Rothchild giraffes on show (there would be even more of them in due course) had been captured in northern Uganda by my younger brother, 'the lionhearted' Richard, at a cost of about one thousand, seven hundred pounds each. They had been in quarantine at our Plymouth Zoo for a year, and some were nearing their maximum height of about seventeen feet. Although multi-course meals of hay, oats, maize, cattle-feed, vegetables and fruit were being fed to them in the splendid custom-built twenty-foot houses that had been created at the edge of the new park, it was noticed, as they got acclimatised, just before the May opening, that they were given to nibbling tender leaves in the higher branches of English oak and beech trees, as well as any available hawthorn around the estate. The giraffes (which live to about twenty years of age) were splendidly young and virile, averaging two to four years. It was hoped to breed from them in due course.

The twelve zebras—two sorts of which had been introduced: the common zebra and the much rarer Hartmann's mountain zebra (of larger size and with a dewlap under his neck)—had been imported at upwards of four hundred pounds each.

Four keepers looked after these animals and the ostriches, which hissed at everyone, as they looked in vain for some sand to bury their heads in!

The official opening of the East African Game Park was attended by the Sixth Marquess of Bath, himself, and he did his stuff, wearing a ten-gallon stetson and astride my African elephant, Wamba. No doubt such showmanship would have delighted some of his illustrious ancestors and would have infuriated others. Certainly, it was a long haul in style (although only fifty years or so in time) since it was one of the butler's first jobs, each weekday morning at Longleat, to iron *The Times* before putting it in the breakfast room, while the parlour maids were busying themselves washing all the coins in the house so that no Thynne hand should be sullied! The cutting-of-the-tape opening ceremony was performed, with equal style, by His Excellency Mr. Jothy Kabuzi, Acting High Commissioner for Uganda, where many of the animals had been trapped eighteen months before.

The Gemsbok (or Oryx gazelle) which had been brought from South Africa, were much admired. A species of antelope, of considerable grace and beauty, they have long, straight horns; the head and legs are black-and-white; and they are mainly mountain creatures, although they adapt easily to level ground. By contrast, the zebras, stunning as they are to look at, can be bad-tempered and stubborn to handle. But we had an odd situation right away, when one male zebra showed embarrassingly amorous inclinations towards the lady visitors, and had to be gently led away.

The assorted game were a fast lot. Ostriches can zoom along at fifty miles per hour, giraffes at thirty miles per hour, and zebras or antelopes can equal horses for speed and endurance.

During the afternoon, two ostriches were scared by a photo-flash, and went belting off into the blue, raising fears that they might charge bodily at a child, or tear at a visitor with their feet. But precautions were decided upon to prevent such a possibility.

Known sometimes as nature's skyscrapers, the giraffes were instantly rated a top attraction. Found only on the African veldt, where their favourite food is the acacia tree, their large dark brown eyes and long black eyelashes give them an appealingly sad expression. They often sleep standing up, since the efforts of lying down and getting up again can make them an easy prey for wild beasts in Africa. But sometimes, fascinatingly, they choose to slumber lying down, with the neck turned backward and the head resting on their rump.

There proved to be no trouble in organising the new game. Land-Rovers were brought into use as sheep-dogs, to get the zebra, eland, ostriches, wildebeest and other game (except for the giraffes) to wherever they were wanted.

Except very rarely, we no longer buy animals from dealers. Richard and John spend part of the year (usually the winter, when the British reserves are quiet) catching or trapping various wild animals, with caring.

Catching a giraffe is tricky. Father has laid it down that the animal must never be chased for more than a minute and a half lest its heart be strained. As I have mentioned, once caught, the animal is taken to a near-by pen and coddled for a month in preparation for the journey. One of the boys also accompanies the animals on the ship and will subsequently 'keep in touch' by paying them frequent visits while they are in quarantine.

So well-adjusted were the new snooty giants at Longleat, indeed, after this kid-glove treatment, that, from the start, each evening, shortly before dusk, they would begin to wind their own way home, led by the herd-leader.

As far as the question of whether the wild animals at Longleat like their new life or not is concerned, father has a lovely little true story he tells. He was out in Uganda with Richard and they had just completed a round-up of giraffes. In the last stages, one of the hunters brought in a giraffe he had named Peter, who was so stunted in growth father took one look and said, 'Send that one back.' Peter was released some miles from the stockade, where the other giraffes were penned, and was forgotten about, until the next morning, when there he was, hammering on the gate to be allowed in. Again he was taken as far as possible from the stockade; again he returned and cried to be let in. So father relented, accepted him, and shipped him.

The sequel to this delightful tale shows that even father can be wrong in selecting animals. Not only is lonely Peter infinitely happier in an English park than he was in the African veldt, but he has shown his gratitude by growing and growing until today he is leader of a herd—head and shoulders above the other males in his group.

Hyenas co-habit reluctantly but fairly peaceably with lions in the wild, holding back at feeding times, but afterwards helping to clear up the mess left by the larger beasts of prey. There would have been advantages in this respect, in having hyenas in the lion reserve at Longleat, and we tried it out hopefully for a time, but it just did not work. We had also thought of putting tigers into the reserve with the lions, but reluctantly we dropped the idea because they were liable to prove too fierce and active; we had also thought of bears, but, although some of them can be embarrassingly affectionate, they can equally be unpredictably vicious.

The picnic area was catching on like a bush fire, with families finding that one of the greatest joys of a smashing day-out was being able to feed themselves while watching the wild game, often only yards away. Picnic baskets proliferated as if the scene was Royal Ascot. The giraffes and zebras had settled in splendidly, the former gliding and floating among the picnickers, their wide eyes ready to spot a tit-bit which would soon de-escalate down their long necks, and the latter approaching visitors boldly, their patterned skins almost too perfect in design to be true. At first it was our wish that people should not feed the game in the East African Park, but this proved impossible to enforce fully and, although it is frowned upon, a certain amount of it goes on. The giraffes, in particular, are difficult to say 'no' to and are cunning at snaffling a little picnic food from here and there, while standing in the same spot, thanks to the length of their 'brass' necks; zebra, too, tend to nuzzle in on picnics and not be repelled.

We don't want to be spoil-sports, or anything, but an expensive giraffe suffering from indigestion (not to say food-poisoning or choking) is a problem we can very well do without.

By the time half-a-million people had passed through the area, the first real mishap occurred in the park, when the fourteen-foot, sixteen-hundredweight young giraffe herd-leader, Peter, galloped over a woman tripper, who was picnicking with two friends, and sent her spinning. Luckily she escaped with bruises. She had gone too close, to take photographs, and the sun glinting in the lens had scared the giraffe. People are warned repeatedly to keep a reasonable distance from the game, which, as I say, are harmless unless badly frightened. The herd galloped after Peter, as they invariably will, but no other damage or casualties resulted. In fact, you can bank on it that about once a month, all seventeen giraffes will have a mad gallop round to let off steam, and the ostriches will act as outriders, but the public—particularly those with cameras—enjoy this and keep far enough away to be safe. Most play safe and snap the scene from inside their cars.

We're absolutely mad about photographs (the Chipperfield–Cawleys) and snap them all the time, so here are one or two simple rules for taking pictures of wild animals from the interior of a motor. The first is to have plenty of film to hand (you'll be really

Simon repels potential invader of chimp island

During the filming of *Casino Royale*, the James Bond film
at Longleat in 1966

Mary paces one of the cheetahs

surprised at how much you need); use medium or fast film and a fast shutter-speed to arrest movement; this will, of course, necessitate a wider aperture; make sure the car windows are clean, and shoot with the lens close to the glass; either drive up fairly close to the animals to be photographed, or, if they are moving at speed, use a telephoto lens.

There can be once-in-a-lifetime opportunities for some to click on a super picture at Longleat. For instance, once in a while a seventeen-foot giraffe will poke his strange head inquisitively towards a camera, presenting the photographer with an almost unique close-up, never available even to safari-hunters in Africa. Then, having satisfied, not to say bemused, another Longleat customer, he will smugly glide away, perhaps to look for some young leaves in a tree, or to join some pals in forming an equally-photographable tall archway of necks, like army swords at a wedding, and magnificent to capture in the setting of an English oak grove.

Many were the celebrities who visited the new park and the lion reserve, sometimes accompanied by their own photographers and publicity men. One of the brighter of the young sparks so to do was Peter Noone (Herman of Herman's Hermits), who, when formally introduced to Marquis, leapt back in mock terror, shouting, 'Get me my agent. There's no *claws* in my contract to cover being eaten by a lion.'

Robert Morley was witty as usual. 'It has been immensely satisfying,' he told me. 'It's difficult to tell what financial effect the Cabinet's mixed-up policies have been having in Rhodesia, but the Chipperfields must be costing South Africa a fortune. By coming here, I feel I've saved at least £1,000 and been as near to wild game as I should ever want to be.'

In the main, I regret to have to say, more women are involved in incidents in the lion park than men. They seem to say to themselves: 'I understand animals. I'm sure these lions really like me.'

G

So they break all the rules; they wind down their windows; they wave handkerchiefs at prides; they even get out of their cars to feed/stroke/kiss the lions, and Mike Lockyer (his early-Hemingway beard bristling) stood rooted to the spot for whole seconds one day at the sight of a housewife pouring orange-squash into a boiling radiator, obviously at the instructions of her husband who was sitting at the wheel watching her. Mike moved and acted fast to prevent what could have been an attack on the woman by one of the least reliable of the lions, but the family were still going on about the car over-heating, not about the danger, after she had been bundled back in and the ever-present breakdown truck summoned.

There are one or two lions who have developed a taste for rubber and would nibble at tyres with their sharp fangs, given half a chance. And the incidence of licked windscreens, bent-back wipers or snapped aerials increases on occasional days when the traffic is heavy, with inevitable hold-ups. Not that anybody complains about such things; rather, it is something people like to savour—a tale from their safari, to be recounted later with zest.

The B.B.C. film, featuring the kapok-filled dummies and showing what could happen to the unwary if they forgot the rules, was scarcely back in its can, after a second showing, when somehow a car got through the reserve gates with camping equipment on its roof. All cars are checked by gatemen before entering the hundred-foot 'tunnel', or fenced entrance-passage, forming, with other gates, a lock at the actual road into the park. The laden car that had somehow, against all precautions, escaped this screening, had not gone many yards in the reserve when a lioness leapt on to its roof, lifted off the equipment and dragged it thirty feet towards the woods, while the family (mum, dad and three children, aged from four to seven, from Crawley, Surrey) watched petrified. In a twinkling, two zebra-painted Land-

Rovers had converged on the scene, and the lioness was persuaded to give up her booty before she had been able to begin shredding it. Even so, a folded tent and a couple of groundsheets had been torn; there were also large teeth-marks in a Lilo. Nothing would persuade the family to have these replaced free, however. Camping gear with lion damage was infinitely more valuable than new equipment. No doubt dad is still drinking out on the tale, and no doubt the kids surreptitiously show the Lilo to friends with many a pulled face and enlarged saucer eyes.

I might have told off the gateman in stronger terms had it not been for the fact that I had driven into an automatic car-wash a few weeks before in my 'eleven six', completely forgetting that I had luggage on the roof, with rather disastrous results.

As an aid to detection and control, high observation-platforms were erected at the entrance points; on busy days, cars were only allowed through the 'lock' gates a dozen at a time; and loud-speakers in the treetops issued warnings to cars even more frequently. If there is a lesson learned, we apply it at once.

But much more disturbing was the incident, a few days after this, when two visitors, on a touring holiday, Robert Andrews, a merchant seaman, and Valerie Jenkins, his girl-friend, both aged twenty-five, and from Bury St. Edmunds, Suffolk, drove into the reserve in a Triumph-Herald coupé. Traffic was fairly heavy, and before long, held up in the valley, the little car caught the attention of Lisa, a somewhat mischievous lioness. While the couple sat petrified, a huge paw suddenly appeared through a gap between the hood and the side-screen on the driver's side, where Miss Jenkins was sitting, unable to move because of cars closely jammed, fore and aft. Lisa then proceeded to claw and chew the canvas vigorously into a *real* hole and, after a moment's reflection, the couple decided they'd rather face the other lions in the open than Lisa in the confined space of the car. So they hopped out sharpish.

The well-tried rescue drills worked perfectly, however, and they were never in any danger. One warden kept the other lions away from the couple while another dealt firmly and effectively with Lisa.

The lesson we learned from this was not to allow soft-topped cars into the enclosure.

Other attractions introduced to the estate generally, by the height of the season (to siphon off some of the crowds heading direct for the lions) including coarse fishing for a few bob a day (with the stipulation that the fish be thrown back); boat trips (with buckets of fish on sale for feeding the Sea-lions); souvenirs (including model African lions, made in Russia, and model Georgian boats, made in Hong Kong); English porcelain lions at four pounds fifty; Longleat-lettered rock; blazer badges commemorating the visit; tea cosies; weighing machines; putting greens; African gift shop; animal skins at seventy-five guineas and upward; vending machines; pin-tables; a garden centre, offering dog kennels, summer houses (two hundred and ten pounds), plaster dwarfs, bunnies, ducks and the like; Pixieland, with lucky Longleat pixies and 'original' Longleat pixie fountains; an answering machine, giving details of the attractions on slips of paper; a dolls' house; a garden-produce stall; three eating places, a bookstall: and the famous Pets' Corner with which, inevitably I was much concerned, and where, currently, I was showing two adorable eight-week-old Russian bear cubs, which were being brought up 'on the bottle' at The Pheasantry, and which were so small I could easily hold one in each hand, as if they were babies' toys. All in all, there was plenty for families to see and do, if they had to wait for an hour or two before visiting the lions.

7

Son of Marquis

I KNEW
that Lady's time was very near, but there is always the worry
with wild creatures that if you interfere with, or even show too
much interest in, an intimate and natural event, like the birth
of cubs, you can disturb the mother emotionally. On the other
hand, a first birth can be treated by a lioness as a sort of dummy-
run for future successes; she can totally ignore her first child
for no reason other than that it is her first; so I had to be on my
toes, to be ready with a feeding-bottle if she did reject Marquis's
first-born, but I equally had to be careful not to show that I
was acting the fussy grandmother, as it were.

It shocks people to learn that lionesses sometimes eat their
young (or, for that matter, that giraffe mothers occasionally
kick their babies to death) but, as any youngster who has kept and
bred rabbits will tell you, it only happens when 'mum' is in an
upset and disturbed state. I therefore talked to Lady as much as
possible when I visited her, trying to reach her ego and get her
into a contented condition, through knowing she was loved.

I also took her for walks, as often as three times per day in the

final stages (explaining to Marquis that his wife needed my attention and that he could jolly well wait until after his babies were
born before expecting a resumption of our daily outings—with
which he seemed to concur fairly serenely). Lady was so heavy
by this time that her 'undercarriage' almost dragged on the
ground; she stooped like a coalman with a hundredweight of
Grade A on his back; and her milk glands were enormously
cumbersome. So the walks were doubly important to keep her fit—
bearing in mind that if she had been in the wild, or even in the
reserve, she would be taking exercise naturally until the last
moment.

I felt her belly a couple of times early in the week I reckoned
the birth was due, and was thrilled to feel the 'electric shock' the
movement of small creatures (or one creature, for that matter)
inside a mother can give. But other than this, I did not interfere
in any way, even to the point of closely looking at her, as I was
dying to do.

Late one night, on my rounds, I was pretty sure I could see
blood dripping from Lady's vagina—a sure sign that her labour
was starting, but she was not moaning, or licking at the blood as
lionesses usually do at this stage, so I could not be absolutely
certain. Marquis and his other two wives were acting normally,
and there was no tension, so, thinking perhaps I was mistaken, I
went off to bed.

Sleep came only fitfully however and at the first chorus of
birdsong, before the sky had fully shaken off the dark, I was out
of bed and on my way to Lady.

Somehow I knew before I reached the mesh, that I had missed
the birth, and I glanced anxiously at Marquis who had come to
greet me, to see what I could read in his face. But he merely
yawned a good morning and left me to peer into the murk
before opening the door. Sure enough, there seemed to be movements in the straw, away from the lionesses, and I thought I

could detect in the gloom that Lady's figure was normal again, as she stood, apparently indifferently, behind the other two, with her back deliberately turned towards me. At a hasty glance, it also appeared that Lady had, as it were, sucked up her milk, withdrawing it into some inner chamber, and had retracted the undercarriage of her teats, so that her glands and nipples seemed utterly barren. The milk would have to be coaxed out of her later, or she would be very sick, but it was very evident that she had decided, as such mothers often do quite naturally, that she would skip the first babies, although she might well decide to become an adoring mother to subsequent litters! Who can explain the workings of a wild woman's heart?

But there was no time to be lost fussing over Lady. I fumbled with the lock, got it open at last, and quickly led Lady and the other two females into another secure 'cage' near by, so that I could investigate the cub or cubs. I then dashed back in and through the straw bedding to the far end, where my eyes could now clearly detect two little spotted bodies limply lying together, showing only flickers of life. Lady had not even bothered to lick them dry after the birth and Marquis did not even seem greatly interested. I knelt down, slapped them soundly to induce some sort of reaction, and gave each the kiss of life until I was sure they were breathing.

I then swept them up in my arms, tucked them under my coat, and rushed them to The Pheasantry.

Marquis, although he looked at me with puzzlement as I slipped out of the building, was evidently not any more interested in fatherhood than Lady was in motherhood, so at least they were a pair in that respect.

Back at the house, I finished off wiping, washing and drying the tiny cubs, while Roger prepared bottles for them, and I cleaned out their eyes, in case they were smarting, before giving them those great cub-comforts—hot-water bottles. They were

maybe eleven inches long, weighing, I would say, between three
and four pounds each. One was female, and the other male, and
the latter was very much livelier than the former. He just had to
be Marquis II, and we decided, in fairness, to call the little girl
Lady II.

Neither cub accepted much milk at the first attempt, but we
persevered and, by the afternoon, both had had a reasonable feed.

In a few days, Marquis II was plump and splendid, beginning
to crawl and stagger around to find out for himself what sort
of world we had brought him into. He was gaining about an
ounce a day and his coat—thicker than Marquis's had been, but
with fewer spots—was shining and upstanding. Lady II, alas, was
still a limp, pathetic bundle of listlessness, who did not seem to
want to move away from the hot-water bottle in her basket,
although we tried all we knew to cheer her up. She had to be fed
lesser quantities, much more often than Marquis Junior, with a
doll's bottle, but we were quite used to this with other cubs. In
bottle-feeding little lions, some say it is best to be guided by the
periods they naturally assume and settle for themselves, but I do
not agree. To me, regular feeding is best for little lions, as it is
for little babies.

As Marquis II's strength grew, so did his curiosity about the
world around him, and in this respect he was certainly a chip off
the old block. He seemed biddable and amiable, as well as being
persistent and self-willed—a fascinating combination that gave
me hope that maybe he would grow up to emulate his dad. He
even softened my heart by putting his little paws around my
neck when I lifted him, in much the way Marquis had done.

Within a couple of weeks, the little bundle of mischief that he
was had developed a tremendous appetite for his fortified milk,
and always kneaded with his paws the plastic baby's bottle to
make sure he got every drop. He was extremely alert at all times,
compared to his sister, and his eyes, still with their blue film, were

focusing sooner. I dug out Marquis's toys for his son, but this was not enough, and his lively taste for play led to 'fun' attacks on shoes, slippers, trouser-legs, stockings, dusters, bits of string, and anything else that happened to be left around. Stalking was his other delight. He would creep up on me, always from the rear, and try to surprise me with a final rush at flying speed. It was Marquis all over again.

In my anxiety that he should not suffer from cat 'flu in the way his father had, I may have over-dosed the little chap with vaccine by mistake, for it made him ill. And, when I was fussing around him that night, fearful lest I had done him harm, his sister died suddenly and silently, without complaint, in her basket alongside. I could have done nothing. She just gasped and was gone. It was terribly sad, and I cried a little, but Lady II just had not wanted to live.

When I was happy again that Marquis's son was again moving from strength to strength, frolicking madly around, or squeezing his fat little tummy into any awkward corner (with Sean, the Great Dane, carrying the cub out of trouble in his mouth, and generally fussing over him) I felt free to resume my normal life again, taking the larger animals for walks, including the un-emotional Marquis (as he had now been proved to be), grooming the horses, getting to know the animals in the new Game Park, and so on.

The week-end after Lady II's death, I flew to Holland to attend the opening of the latest Chipperfield enterprise: a very beautiful and attractively laid-out seventy-five-acre lion park at Tilburg, prepared by my father, in partnership with the Tilburg City authorities. I took with me Major, the cross-eyed lion who had been Roger's favourite cub when Marquis Senior had been mine. With Major I made a number of appearances, in person and on television, to publicise the new reserve.

Fortunately the disciplines and restrictions, learned from hard experience at Longleat, had been instilled in the staff at Tilburg, reinforced by a couple of English wardens, because, in a rival park in Holland, with less experience, a Finnish tourist with a physical disability was dragged from his invalid car by a young lion, which managed to open the sliding door.

The ultimate in idiocy, in this sort of way, had happened at Longleat one day when I was away, and Roger went quite pale at the memory when he came to tell me about it.

It had happened, fortunately, after the lions had been fed and when they were mostly drowsy, or having a snooze. It underlined the fact that wardens, even at Longleat, have to be just as vigilant at quiet times. On this occasion, a patrol, rounding the corner at Born Free Valley, came upon a man standing a few yards away from his car and calmly throwing stones at a recumbent pride, less than a dozen yards away from him. When he had been whisked away to the office, as a nut-case, and questioned, the man said calmly that he had been doing it to rouse the lions, 'so that I could get a more realistic picture'. It makes you wonder—it really does—which have the higher intelligence—people or animals.

Soon after I got back from Holland, I developed the symptoms (which are very unpleasant) of ringworm. I had obviously caught it from young lions I had been handling and treating there, and, alas, I passed it on to Marquis. Thereafter, for three weeks or so, we both had to have the same treatment—grisovin tablets and a ghastly purple spray—several times a day. I'll draw a veil over this nasty (but not too serious) disease, which is so hard to get rid of, and it lasted eight weeks in our case. I felt even more sorry for my lion than for myself, for ringworm looks very much worse than it is, and the hair came off poor Marquis's coat in rings. That, plus a tick he got in his ear when we were away filming in Dakar (which was just as difficult to shift), was the only serious illness Marquis had had since his terrible life-and-death struggle against feline enteritis, when he was six months old, I am happy to say. And we were both able to potter about and do some work, despite the ringworm scourge, which strangers tended to regard like the plague.

Towards the end of July, more or less fully recovered, I flew to Dusseldorf in the Ruhrland area, for the opening of our latest venture, a German lion park at Buer, near Gelsenkirchen. This reserve had been set up as a fifty-fifty partnership deal with a charming and somewhat eccentric millionaire-landowner, and aristocrat, known as the Graf, or to give him his full name, the Graf Westerholt. There had been problems in this case. The town authorities at Gelsenkirchen had raised various objections, which were eventually overcome, but which necessitated, among other things, the incorporation of electrified fences. The local council for the protection of natural beauties also had a go at us and said the lions would destroy the trees in the woodlands in the estates. We were able, of course, from our unique experience, to point out that, while native deer, which roamed free in the area, were very destructive in this way, lions emphatically were not!

The reserve covered about seventy acres in all; admission was the equivalent of one pound; we had introduced forty lions, and three experienced 'white hunters' from Longleat. In the event, it became a very big success for the Graf and for us.

The imminent laying-out of four hundred and fifty acres of the Duke of Bedford's splendid estate at Woburn as a one-and-a-half million pound wild-life park was announced the same Saturday as the German reserve opened. The animals for the famous top-of-the-stately-pops estate, just off the M1 motorway—including white rhinos, lions, zebras, giraffes and monkeys—were already in quarantine, and my brother, Richard, was getting ready to take over this second vast English project. As at Longleat, the new venture was a fifty-fifty deal between my father and the Duke. It was undoubtedly a major triumph for the former, because (a)

Longleat and Woburn had previously been cut-throat competitors, and (b) Woburn, without the animals, had long been rated far-and-away the greatest commercial success of its kind in the whole world.

As the long, hot August of 1968 went on and on, even the African lions at Longleat began to complain about the heat by becoming less and less active and by taking to lying on their backs, like large mink-coloured dogs, with their legs in the air— this during the periods when they would normally be moving around among the cars, which was not good enough—not fair to the cash customer. To pep them up a bit (and it worked with the young ones) a play-park for lions was introduced, with old tree-trunks to play on and sloping ramps leading to a high platform on stilts.

Aboard the animal conveyor-belt called The Pheasantry, where the sun was less disturbing, Marquis II had been joined by several other rejected 'babies' from the estate. Cubs love to invent games, and indeed must be kept amused to prevent them turning their energies to destructive ends. All David's and Charles's old discarded toys were fortunately available to the cubs. A solid plastic football gave them a great deal of pleasure, because it rolled so fast and so easily. Sometimes one of the cubs would take a flying leap and plop with its belly on top of the ball, slide a few yards, then end up on its back with its feet in the air— lamb-like in his frizzy coat of knotty wool. By the time it had recovered, one of the other cubs would have snatched the ball and would have rolled it away underneath a table, there to guard it, hissing and spitting at any threats to take it from him. After a time this villain would get fed-up with playing by himself and would pretend to look away so that one of the others could get the ball for the game to begin all over again.

Mischievous games of hide-and-seek would take place between us and them, with the space behind our long curtains in the sitting-room top-favourite hiding place; but only by the slight movements of squat paws did we know how many were hidden; and, when found, the cubs impishly dashed off to look for another cover, in high hopes that the human would be daft enough to keep up the game all day.

We carefully manicure our cubs' nails while they are living in the house, to avoid pulled threads on the furnishings, on which they still try, while stretching at the same time, to sharpen them again.

Visitors are always willing to nurse the cubs but this is seldom allowed to last long. In a moment, a wriggly body will go plop on the floor and its owner will shoot off in a sideways scamper, hell-bent on exploring the world. Occasionally, we have cubs who want to be nursed all the time, whereupon discouragement from such weakness, together with prodding into lively action, is the administered medicine.

Marquis II, who had developed his dad's habit of pensively sucking the end of his tail, was different from any of the others in that he would approach visitors with dignity as well as curiosity, and would reject as many as he nuzzled and accepted, after a cursory look.

Charles, the chimp, had taken rather a liking to young Marquis, and would show it by bopping the little lion on the nose to say 'Come and have a game'. They would then play dirt-tracks in a skidding race around the furniture, until 'Junior', tongue out and panting hard, would nip the chimp, whereupon Charles would sulk, or go off to look for David.

Inevitably, it fell to me to exercise the young ones, as well as some of their parents, and I would lead the cubs out into the soft Wiltshire mornings, where the air was pungent with the smell of badger, fox, rabbit and field-mouse. The cubs would go absent-without-leave, if I gave them half a chance, to indulge in wild hunting forays among the trees, or they would tumble, in full cry, after a gaggle of birds, forcing them to wing, and doubtless expecting that, if they chased hard enough, one would fall out of the sky.

Mostly I took them into the nearest patch of woodland, where one or two would inevitably fall down deep burrows (to the accompaniment of hysterical laughter from me) to emerge sheepishly, their little faces screwed up in disgust and their silky coats plastered with earth.

I sentenced them to terms of tethering for their repeated misdemeanours; I raised my voice to a pitch which frightened even me; I threatened to walk them on the chain; but I went on laughing until the return and the grooming that proved necessary. During this, they would pretend to bite me, but even at this age (seven, eight and nine weeks) their nips in play could really hurt.

Gradually, the cubs' characters were emerging. More and more, Marquis II was shaping up like his father, head and shoulders above the others—open, honest and intelligent; but Sally, for instance (the nearest in age to him of the others) was totally different, and more average, as a cub—inclined to be introverted and sly. Under a guise of innocence, she slunk cunningly. When Marquis Junior was following me about to see if he could help with anything, she would have tiptoed off to curl up in old Marquis's rocking chair or any other comfortable corner where she would be unlikely to be discovered. She could also be the ringleader when mischief was about.

One thing they all had in common, however, was that, after an hour or so in the woods, they would have their feeds and would then collapse into their various baskets, to fall instantly into the deepest of sleep, until the next buffet meal was due, while I had to go straight into some other routine, still (as always) involving animals.

The day soon came when Marquis II, like his father, had to begin earning his keep, if he was to remain at the Pheasantry and not be sent out to the reserve. So, one day, accompanied by Yula, the Alsatian bitch, he appeared at a Birmingham store and created a furore, with vast crowds oohing and ahhing, and with reporters asking people present for their reactions to the 'royal' visitor, and with a small boy being taken away, crying to break his heart, because he could not take Marquis II home. His plump spotted body, with its rolls of puppy fat, was patted brown and white (or whatever the lion equivalent is of black and blue); as if he was John Bull in *Punch*, his tail was twisted; he got bubbles up his nose from a bath a naked model was taking; he was offered English cheese and French champagne; perfume was atomised over him; gloves were put on his paws and a tiara on his head; and throughout he acted like the great and good young gentleman he was, suppressing his yawns as well as his squeaks. Here was— dared I think—Marquis all over again. I was certainly very proud of him.

From about this time on, when I took little Marquis along to open fêtes, jumble-sales, shops and the like, if they had a microphone, I would get him to give his little roar (which he had begun to spring on us like a child offering an adult a jack-in-the-box) as an official means of officially declaring the event open. And many's the inch of newspaper space this simple idea commanded for the cub and for Longleat.

8

. . . and Manfred made three

SUDDENLY, AT
the beginning of September, we had trouble at Half-Mile Pond,
the beautiful stretch of water created by the damming of the
River Wylie, little more than a millstream hereabouts.

Surprisingly, the gentle hippopotamuses were the villains of
the piece for once. There had been daily battles between the
chimps and the seals, but this had been part of the fun for the
visitors. Trouble with the two-and-a-half ton hippos was altogether another matter. Expected to breed for us, from about the
age of six, and to live to thirty-five or forty years, our three young
hippos, all under five, were getting through enormous quantities of
hay, grass, root vegetables, bread and fruit, and had proved to be
generally extremely docile, not to say lethargic, wallowing most
of the time in the 'mud, mud, glorious mud' of their strongly-
constructed pens.

But now voluminous passions were at work; a bloated eternal
triangle had unwittingly reared its ugly head in the *ménage*.

We had started, as I mentioned earlier, with a pair of hippos,
named Arnold (a magnificent specimen, aged five) and Freda, a

Suzanne's 'dolls'

The kick off

real plump young dolly-bird, who could have stood-in splendidly for 'two-ton' Janet Webb, in the Morecambe and Wise show on television. But, after their popularity had been established, we had introduced hippo number three to the others—Manfred, a four-year-old, painfully shy and quiet creature, who should, theoretically, have fitted splendidly into the settled pattern.

But even a hippo will turn, albeit slowly, and we had now reached the point where Manfred was kicking against the pricks, so to speak, at having to play gooseberry, while the other two spooned and flirted noisily and outrageously. For a time, Manfred was off his food, only demolishing nineteen hundredweights or so to his rival's ton, which was bad enough. But eventually there came a day when Freda and Arnold made it plain to poor Manfred that, as far as they were concerned, he could get lost—which is what he did.

To our astonishment, for the pits had been carefully planned and constructed, Manfred escaped from his pen into the open waters of the lake, by tunnelling deep into the mud and surfacing when he had bored beyond the concrete walls (I tell you, even the Wooden Horse is nothing to the goings-on at Longleat!) When he had reached deep water, Manfred then began to give a great display of careless abandon—diving and surfacing like a porpoise and emitting great snorts of independent disgust.

In addition to the crowds of enthralled spectators who witnessed Manfred's exhibitionist performance from the safety of surrounding slopes, the colony of sea-lions had a much closer view of the action, to the alarm of some of them. All were young seals, under two years of age, and as they had been shipped in wet tanks from Californian seas, they had certainly seen nothing like an all-action, swimming-diving-snorting hippo before.

Some of the chimps on the island, who were entranced by their ring-side view, may have lived with hippos in Africa, but as

H

non-swimmers they were very impressed and were soon applauding the finer points of the performance.

Try as we liked, we could not catch Manfred, or entice him back, and there was nothing for it but to withdraw the safari boats (and the visitors) from these suddenly-dangerous waters. Fortunately, the lake was fenced, which kept Manfred from wandering off among the paying customers at the big house, but all we could do was to leave open the massive gate to his pen, and lay out a double supper for him, in the hope that he would return when he was hungry.

Sure enough, the next morning, having cooled, he decided to turn the other cheek (or is it jowl in his case?) and return home in the interests of breakfast. At once, there was a brief *fracas*, in which husky Arnold, the hipper (or hippier) of the two male hippos, gave Manfred a bit of a trouncing, and in which the latter got the worst of the argument with young Freda, also. But after a period of sulking, Manfred decided it was better to be a well-fed wallflower than a soppy lover-boy, anyway.

A new vaccine developed to control feline enteritis had been produced at Bristol, and three of my lion cubs were the first such animals in the country to be inoculated with it. Known as Katavac, it was claimed to be a revolutionary advance in this all-important field, and I wondered, as I held the cubs, if Marquis might have been saved the terrible illness he had suffered as a child if the new drug had been available then. Cat 'flu is the scourge of the feline world (be they wild or domestic animals) and causes me more worry than any other factor in looking after lions. One, to me, all-important feature of the new treatment is that one shot is all that is needed to make an animal immune to the disease that kills thousands of the country's eight million cats every year. Previous vaccines (as I very well know) had had to be supplemented by booster injections about once per year. This one was not one hundred per cent, on one injection, but it was as near

as dammit. Dr. Ronald Johnson, of the Bristol School of Veterinary Science, had helped develop this important new product,
having isolated the disease on tissues taken from the spleen of
various animals we had sent him (plus animals from Bristol Zoo)
which had suffered from the disease, and died from it, although
(like Marquis) they had been inoculated against it.

About this time another Noah Chipperfield's Ark (the Clan
McIntyre, to give its Sunday go-to-meeting name) had arrived at
Avonmouth, with a cargo of elephants, giraffes, rhino, wildebeest, elands, ostriches, gazelles, impalas, water-bucks and oryx—
about seventy animals in all—some labelled 'Woburn', but many
designed to increase the attractions at Longleat. Unloaded in
fly-proof nets, most of the creatures were due to spend twelve
months in quarantine in our zoo at Plymouth, but, there being
no such restrictions then, the elephant and rhino were freed at
once.

Simultaneously, in mid-September, another load of well-
shaped meat descended gracefully on us all. Marquis was very
much present, as was the Marquess (*and* Roger Cawley, blast him)
when Harlech TV held the finals of their beauty contest at
Longleat. The object was to find the prettiest girl in Wales and
the West, to be named and honoured as Miss Harlech for the
following year. Twelve gorgeous girls eventually lined up on an
improvised cat-walk in swimsuits, with number plates on their
wrists, and I thought back to the not-so-long-ago days when I had
been a beauty queen in the area myself, in the Miss Bournemouth
Belle Stakes.

'Girls, girls, girls—the loins of Longleat', the current compère
punned in a tome of reverent lechery, mixed with patronising
gallantry. Lord Harlech, once famed as an escort of the widowed
Jacqueline Kennedy, also stood around looking as someone else
had it, 'like a spare peer at Smithfield', and Lord Bath joined a
jury of quasi-eminent people, who included Sir Gerald Nabarro

(of motoring fame); David Hughes, the singer; Kiki Dee, the vocalist; and Bobby Butlin, from a rival animal-less camp establishment. When it came to the bit, Lord Harlech covered himself with embarrassment by putting the winner's sash on upside down, while Marquis, who had been introduced to excite the girls, playfully nipped at Craig Douglas's heels, as the crooner prepared to serenade the winner, and I failed to restrain Marquis, so convulsed was I with laughter. Not since the Rolling Stones gave a concert at Longleat, in pre-lion days, had there been such a madly non-regal occasion at the Thynne ancestral homestead.

Generally speaking, life was never dull at Longleat, and soon after the beauty contest there came the hair-raising and milk-curdling saga of Marquis's encounter with Mickey, the lion-hearted white mouse. If this had any significance, it probably was that it tended to prove that, whatever a lion is, it is not a big cat. For the record, this was early October, 1968, and Marquis, at two years, eight months, weighed in at around three hundred and sixty pounds, with muscles to match, and a head six times as big as mine, physically speaking; but he was still, in some ways, a great big, adorable, over-grown puppy-cub.

I had been asked to train a lion and a mouse for a film built around the appropriate Aesop's fable. Naturally, no lion would do but Marquis. And I soon located a pet mouse that was full of personality and still young enough to be trained. When I intro-duced them for the first time, in the office at The Pheasantry, the little mouse (who inevitably became known as Mighty Mickey) faced the large lion manfully and cheerfully. I had been teaching Mickey some tricks, with the result that, almost instantly, he decided to show off to Marquis by performing acrobatics within inches of my lion's twitching nose. This did not go down too well, and my friend's mane hackles went up instinctively; his mouth also opened, either in astonishment or in preparation for a roar. At that Mickey hopped forward and not only gazed into the jaws of death, but for one breath-stopping instant appeared to be about to jump into them.

If Marquis was truly a cat, then I had obviously failed him by not explaining to him how cats are expected to react to their enemy, the mouse. As Mickey sprang playfully to one side and accidentally landed on one of the lion's enormous forepaws, Marquis panicked and leapt backwards, like a big daft tumphie, fastidiously avoiding any danger of stepping on the minute white morsel cart-wheeling before him. Indeed, unless I was mistaken, the mighty lion was actually quaking with fear at the antics of the infinitesimal mouse. It was the saga of the robin redbreast all over again, in blanched form.

Marquis's most relaxed moment, in his first rehearsal, came when Mickey sat on his head, but this was probably because he couldn't feel the tiny body through the layers of thick black mane. Even then, the mouse smartly upstaged the lion by calmly sitting back on his haunches and washing his face.

Days later, when Marquis was covered by a net in the woods, Mickey on his head, and the cameras about to turn, it was still the former who was scared of the latter, and cross-eyed as well, now he knew where the white mouse was squatting.

Marquis was doing it just for me, but, in truth, he did not like it one little bit.

It was nearing the end of what had been known in industry as 'Quality and Reliability Year', and, one December day, it seemed to me that few firms could have deserved the Queen's Award for packaging more than good old Kodak.

We had been urgently awaiting the arrival of some processed colour transparencies of Marquis and Mickey, the white mouse. A selection of the ten best was to be made to be sent on at once to America, where they were urgently required for a major magazine article, which we hoped would carry a plug or two for our newly-opened lion park at Miami, Florida.

There was a deadline to keep, via a quick dash to London airport and the conveyance of the package to New York in the pocket of an airline-captain friend; and we had learned over the years never to fall down on Press deadlines. So we were all on the look-out for the postman that morning—having telephoned the day before, and learned that the transparencies had gone off O.K. When the usual time passed, with no sign of a parcel, we brooded, but there was work to be done that could not wait, so we pressed on, having forgotten completely that the Christmas season was so near that casual post-office staff had been recruited, even for our semi-remote area.

The result was that the next thing I knew, as I moved towards the outside tap, to water my horses, was that all the dogs were barking warnings, which were taken up by the cubs and, last of all, the elephant and the horses. It was such a dreadful commotion that I dropped the bucket and ran helter-skelter to see what was going on. As I rounded the corner of the stables leading into the main yard, spray flying from my boots, I just caught a glimpse of a young lad, in blue and red piping, zooming across the cattle-grid and down the approach road on his bicycle, as if all the bats of hellfire-corner were after him. I had never seen him before; he was obviously a temporary postman.

Roger had come out of the office at the same moment, equally puzzled by the row. And all was immediately clear to both of us. Because we had delayed over breakfast, waiting for the post, I had been too late to take Marquis for his walk. Rather than have him think I had forgotten our routine, I had taken him out of the harem and had chained him in the yard, rather nearer to where I would be working. He knew by this that the morning outing was postponed, rather than cancelled. This happened often enough for the regular postman to be quite used to Marquis, and vice-versa. But the young lad on his bike had probably never seen a lion before, certainly not as close as that, so that when Marquis walked forward to the extent of his chain, to greet him, the lad had simply thrown his mail in the air and departed, shouting in fear.

This had made the animals 'create'. But, worse, it had allowed the still-mischievous Marquis to get hold of the Kodak package and investigate it, lest there was a tasty bite inside, so that, by the time I had snatched it from his mouth, there were teeth-holes through the wrapping-paper. But, by a miracle, the Kodak dispatcher had used a stout tin to ensure safe delivery, and this had blunted Marquis's inquisitive attacks long enough for the precious contents to be safe when I rescued them.

The dent-holes in the tin, made by Marquis's fangs just before I had managed to snatch it away, reminded me of a story told me by the pest-control expert sent to examine The Pheasantry for dry rot, wet rot, and such things, just before we moved in.

'I'm an animal trainer, too,' he confessed, as he poked about in a beam and found woodworm. 'I have a marvellous formula for making these little beggars pack their bags.

'But, do you know,' he went on, 'potential customers used to send us samples of their pests when asking for a quotation. In the case of woodworms, we had to appeal to everyone to pack them in tins. The trouble was, we were constantly receiving, through the post, *empty* matchboxes riddled with holes.'

I suppose it's bad enough that the postmen who serve us have to slither down lanes gooey with mud, negotiate bumpy cattle-grids, plough through thorns, and open and close a number of gates, without also having to cross the dangerous wild-animal-infested 'jungle' named 'the yard'—all this perhaps to deliver a bundle of bills; a special offer of free L.P.s to anyone prepared to sign an agreement to pay sixty-six pence per week for twenty-three years for endless bargain discs; an invitation to open a fête in Tillietoodlum, Kirkcudbrightshire, or some such convenient village; and leaflets offering advice on how to raise cats and dogs healthily.

9

Diamonds and manure

I HAD recently been involved again in carting blocks of frozen water to Iceland, in that I had to convey a menagerie of mainly African animals to French West Africa for a film, and Marquis had been one of them.

The destination was the impressive but steamy seaport of Dakar, and the film was an Anglo-French production, *Southern Star*, with Ian Hendry and Ursula Andress.

The joke about this one was that, whereas Marquis was provided with a stand-in, I had to do all the difficult bits for Miss Andress; considering I'm what is known as 'petite' and she has made her name in a more 'upstanding' way, this seemed neither right nor fair (as they say of the left leg of a Zulu).

Anyway, my coals to Newcastle cargo, from Longleat to Dakar, consisted of three lions (the other two being untrained ones chosen straight from the reserve for their good looks and sweet tempers); two ostriches; twenty baboons; two cobras; and my leopard, Chico. I also had three of the 'lads' with me—Roy, Ginger and Snaky.

The plot was a typical jungle-style adventure, with everybody chasing a stolen diamond. At one stage the jewel had to be swallowed by one of my ostriches, which was easy enough to achieve by means of a piece of preserving sugar, and there was a dizzy moment when (in my role as Ursula Andress) I was galloping across the veldt, in pursuit of the ostrich, in full evening dress.

But it was probably the 'lads' who provided the funniest moments. Roy and Ginger were given small parts as 'natives'— the former riding an ostrich, and the latter up a tree with Chico, the leopard. They did their stuff splendidly, but it was hilarious to see them 'blacked up' for their roles, because Roy is a blond and Ginger is a carrot-top!

'Snaky' Williams (who now looks after the baboons at Longleat) was equally a riot in that, when he'd had a few drinks, he would get his cobras out of their boxes and put them through all their tricks in the cocktail bar of the poshest hotel in Dakar, to the utter astonishment of the residents.

Marquis's part called for him to be shot after a chase through the undergrowth, culminating in a giant leap towards the man with the gun. I had practised this for weeks beforehand at The Pheasantry by making him jump many times towards me, from a pedestal, over the top of a 'lad' impersonating the cameraman. The result was that, when the time came, Marquis was bang-on super-duper the line-perfect film star coming in on cue and 'rising' like the King he is, to the occasion.

I'd like to say he also gave up the ghost in splendidly moving fashion, like George Sanders at his best (or even George Raft) but, instead, this poignant moment was left to his stand-in. When Marquis had leapt over the cameraman towards the hunter, every ripple of his magnificently muscled body recorded on film, he went off to his quarters to drink a few gallons of water and chew a bone or two. The director then cut to a shot of the stand-in lion, from the 'crowd' in the Longleat reserve, which was lying beside the hunter, tranquillised and smothered in tomato ketchup.

No sooner had the film ended than we were in trouble, when a typical African coup took place—mainly bloodless, but alarming enough while it lasted. The rebels successfully overthrew the government and immediately seized the airport, with the result that we were all stranded in a decaying town in tropical heat.

Father had been out with us during part of the two months we had been at work, and the fact that he was cut off from the world, at a time of rapid growth in our business, was serious indeed. He was, in fact, due in America on a tightly-arranged schedule of business conferences. So we risked the rebels' bullets and drove through the guarded streets to the airport, where somehow dad talked himself into occupying the co-pilot's seat on the very last plane out before the runways were blown up. Maybe the fact that he was a very successful fighter pilot in the war had something to do with this piece of one-upmanship. Anyway, the rest of us just had to cool our heels until things settled down again in Dakar a couple of weeks later, by which time the problems at home were multiplying like the lions in our park in Holland (which in a couple of words, is 'almost embarrassingly').

Just before the start proper of the 1969 season at Longleat, the entrance gates to the lion reserve were improved by the mounting of seven life-sized steel lions. These had been designed by a friend of the Thynnes who had once had a farm in East Africa and who certainly had a true eye for a lion; and they were made by a sixty-six-year-old blacksmith, Phillip Blake, in the quiet little village of Broughton. He was an old pal of ours—a 'smith since he was twelve—who had made all the cages for our Southampton Zoo (which involved the use of three miles of electric welding-rods) as well as the special bath for our crocodile, and other such jobs. His work for Longleat had now resulted in a major export order for the animal park at Royal Palm Beach, Miami, Florida.

In all, Phillip Blake had, in fact, been making miscellaneous bits and pieces for the Chipperfields for over fifty years (including such items as specially weighted steel cups for a tightrope-walker to balance a pole on the end of his nose, or, recently, the delicately fashioned stand for Gina Fossett's trapeze act). He had got into this off-beat line through having been at school with my father, which must have been quite an experience.

Just before Easter, plans were announced to open a three-hundred-acre park near Dublin, in conjunction with the famous Slazenger family, of sporting fame, and 'with lions as fearsome as the donkeys in Connemara,' as the *Irish Times* put it. The result was that I went by air from Bristol with father on a visit to Powerscourt, the magnificent estate of Ralph Slazenger and his wife near Dublin. We took the three-month-old Marquis III with us in a basket (Marquis having become a father again, through Countess) to sniff out the land for the lions we hoped would follow. Powerscourt occupies thirteen thousand acres at Enniskerry, County Wicklow, and, although we only proposed to use three hundred acres for the lion reserve, we were met by a ten-man protest group carrying posters saying: 'The Land for the People' and 'Small farmers IN. Animals OUT'. Marquis III was more upset by the noise than any of us. The 'delegates' said the Lands Commission should have acquired the estate to run as a co-operative. They listened to our points of view with courtesy, I must say, as is often the way with the Irish, and, after Mrs. Slazenger had moved among them asking if any of them were personally involved in agriculture, we explained that the reserve could employ far more country people than it could possibly support on agriculture, and it all passed off fairly well.

Back at The Pheasantry, my horse Jarro happened to be in the yard one morning, waiting patiently to be exercised, when Marquis

III, who was happily shaping up like a miniature of his brother and father, waltzed along looking for new ways of being naughty. No sooner had I turned my back to get Jarro's saddle than the little lion started to attempt an ascent of the horse's near-fore leg. At once the little claws dug in and the latest baby Marquis had scarcely reached the horse's nobbly knee when a startled muzzle pushed itself in astonishment into Marquis's cold nose, and Jarro emitted one of the most explosive snorts I have heard from a horse, simultaneously leaping backwards into an incongruous splay-legged position. Had I not leapt just as quickly towards him, almost doubled up with laughter, he would have been off into the blue. I soon calmed him and attempted to introduce him formally to the latest 'title-holder', for he had always been on very good terms with the first Marquis. But meanwhile, the little lion, having been thrown in the air a considerable distance when the horse had sprung back, was now looking a trifle dazed at the violence of the adventure. And, alas, each was now somewhat suspicious of the other, so that I doubted if I would ever be able to teach Marquis III the rare circus trick of leaping from a platform on to Jarro's back, which his father had uniquely achieved almost two years before.

When the calendar showed it to be a matter of days until Easter, which would bring with it the great stampede of cars with which the season gets going at Longleat, we repainted our signs, oiled our turnstiles and carefully re-counted our lions, ready for the rush.

A mobile office of the R.A.C. had now been strategically placed in the park to help motorists, but for some reason the giraffes took a liking to the Club's caravan and kept poking their long noses in, with the result that customers, when they arrived, often had to elbow seventeen-foot nosy-parkers aside to get to the counter.

One day, impossibly busy though we were, we took time off

to welcome and chat to George Mottershead, the brilliant animal expert who founded Chester Zoo forty years ago, and who helped us a great deal in the early days on questions of animal and human safety. We also owe to him the idea of Man–Ape Island, but we are not alone in this. One of his great successes at Chester was in pioneering methods of keeping chimpanzees alive, well, cheerful, and breeding. The first chimp shot into space might not have got off the ground had it not been for Mr. Mottershead. When planning this world-shattering flight, the American authorities asked around to find out where the world's happiest chimps were—on the grounds that only a contented animal would react normally in orbit—and they were told the answer was Chester Zoo. So they visited it and reproduced Mr. Mottershead's island hides as homes for space-pioneering chimps.

During April, 1969, repairs had also proved necessary to the five miles of road that snaked through the lion park. More than half-a-million cars and buses had left their mark in the three years since the Longleat project was first launched upon a bemused but enthusiastic British public.

Two young experts, Rodney Hughes and Ken Walton, both from near-by Midsomer-Norton, got down to work to make new the much-punished tar-macadam. Watching over them were one foreman (Ken's brother, Alan), one 'white hunter' with rifle, and nearly fifty lions.

They worked hard and well, but productivity was hardly aided by the lions sniffing around the tar, and not because it's supposed to cure asthma, either!

Later in the month, not for the first time since Longleat went over to wild animals, a stately row was brewing at the highest levels, this time via the William Hickey column of the *Daily Express*. The mighty Duke of Marlborough (by then in his early seventies) having previously run down the idea of lions in ancestral homes, made an announcement that he would open his stately hothouses at Blenheim Palace to the public, whereupon the Marquess of Bath, ever the humorous and generous friend, offered the duke a considerable quantity of lion dung for his use in the new project, with apologies for the vulgar name of the fertilising material.

Marlborough at once replied (making the nomenclature of the material under discussion slightly less 'common' in the process). 'Lord Bath suggests I use lion manure for the propagation of my plants. Having shot these fine animals in Kenya, and knowing them to be the smelliest ever, I feel I should qualify myself as a recipient of the Order of the Bath.'

The Duke of Bedford (now becoming a lion-man at Woburn, under the guidance of my brother Richard) could not resist the opportunity for an aristocratic riposte and a bit of publicity: 'I should have thought,' he giggled, 'that manure is the perfect subject for the Duke of Marlborough to talk about. He may say we're vulgar, but I say there's simply nothing original about the man. Even his garden centre is not original. *My* garden centre opened months ago!'

Getting in on the mêlée, Viscount Camrose's head gardener at the famous Hackwood Park estate, near Basingstoke, Hants, Harry van Zomeren, explained that he knew about this type of compost, having previously worked around the private zoo of gambling-club owner, John Aspinall, and having experimented with tiger's manure on plants, only to have them die off as a result. 'I am convinced,' he concluded firmly, 'that all dung from carnivorous animals is absolutely deadly for plants . . .'

I wouldn't know, never having tried it. There is, however, a splendid wisteria tree in The Pheasantry garden which has been favoured by successive Marquises for their jets, and, astonishingly, it is still alive and healthy. There appears to be, in fact, a special use for lion dung which none of the *Express*'s correspondents seemed to have thought of. After the Hickey affair, a Highland laird wrote and asked us to supply him with lion dung, which we have been doing ever since. Apparently when the deer are threatening to damage his young trees, he hangs bags of the stuff near by. This effectively keeps the deer away from that part of the park for three or four weeks, after which a fresh supply of the smelly stuff has to be hung there. And that's quite enough on so 'vulgar' a topic.

It may be interesting to the many who tend to knock Britain to know that, in our line of business at least, British workers are best. We send key men (and women) from here to all our overseas parks. And when we began to advertise in April 1969 for grooms to look after giraffes, zebras, antelopes and ostriches, we mentioned that there would be opportunities to travel the world to our other parks, which indicated that we were thinking of adding East African game to our lion reserves abroad—which we were.

All our 'white hunters', who are tough professionals, believe me, have their favourite 'true' stories about animals, which they tell in their caravans over a drink, and the one I like best is the most far-fetched one.

It seems that one of the fully-grown lions in the Miami park fell into the swimming pool and all but drowned. An intrepid warden dived in, struggled to the side with the non-swimming, three-hundredweight beast, yanked him out single-handed, and, almost with his (the warden's) last breath, began artificial respiration. This had no results, so in desperation the exhausted 'hunter' resorted to the kiss of life; whereupon, miracle of miracles, the lion came round.

'My dear chap,' my father is alleged to have said to him afterwards, 'did you not notice the danger when you put your head in his mouth?' 'No,' was the reply, 'you couldn't notice anything but its bad breath!'

There were always people reporting sightings of our lions at various distances from Longleat; and, indeed, when *any* wild animal was reported to have been seen almost anywhere in the south, the local police would think of us and 'phone us automatically—a compliment in one way; a nuisance in others. I now logged a call from Bath police that Mr. Christopher Robinson had seen a lioness (he had even observed its sex) run across a straight stretch of road, as he was driving along it, at Kingsdown. A patrol from Corsham had been investigating but had found nothing, other than a fox's lair. Had we lost a lion? We counted carefully (for the umpteenth time in three years) and rang back to say that they were all present and correct. It was just another item in our carefully-kept log-book. Although we do not expect ever to be noting a genuine escape by a lion, we believe in playing safe and investigating everything.

In June, the International Lions' Club, which has nothing to do with lions, really, but raises money for charity and for needy individual cases, approached us for the use of a lion at fund-raising gatherings in the course of the twelve months following, the first event to be at Basingstoke's carnival-week procession in June. I decided to use the twelve-month-old Marquis II for this major series of occasions, and the Lions backed the scheme with a hundred thousand pounds of accident-liability insurance. One idea was that, in street processions, Marquis II would ride uncaged on the back of a specially dressed lorry as a major attraction.

This was nothing compared to many stunts we had been up to in the past, but, as sometimes happens, local (to me, blind) opposition killed the entire scheme dead. Although the Basingstoke Carnival Committee had given its unqualified blessing, the Lions' Club were warned by the police that court action was possible if they went ahead. Chief Superintendent Wilfred Burton of Basingstoke said: 'We think this is a very unwise thing to do, and it may be constituting an offence under the Cruelty

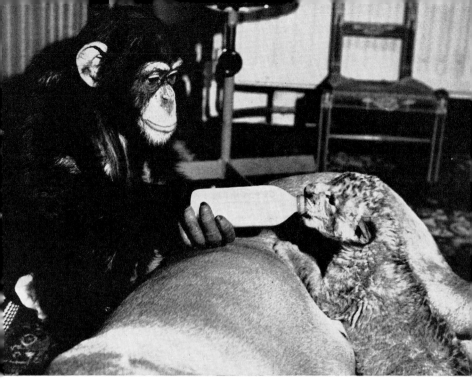

Nanny Charles

Mary examines a tranquillised injured lion from the Reserve

Meals on wheels

Springtime at Longleat

to Animals Act in certain circumstances. We are keeping the matter well under consideration.'

This really made me bristle. Cruelty to animals, indeed!

The local club secretary was marvellous. Pointing out that young Marquis had already taken part in a carnival at Sheffield, totally uncaged, he said: 'We are going ahead despite police opposition.'

Whatever happened, the publicity was good for the local Lions' Club and the carnival (which would result in a procession of seventy-five floats and a street crowd of twenty thousand), but we firmly promised to help fight the case if the police took action, believing that they were bluffing. Alas, before the first carnival was to be held, the Lions chose to climb down. Said our secretary, 'Our club is composed of members who have a high sense of civic responsibility, and while, of course, we would have liked to have had the lion in the parade, we would not do so without the fullest approval of the authorities. We were assured by Longleat that everything would have been quite in order, and there would not possibly have been any question of cruelty to the animal or a risk to public safety.'

The R.S.P.C.A. had of course supported police objections. They did this partly on the fairly sensible grounds that people would be throwing coins at the floats and some of them might strike the lion (although the R.S.P.C.A. people failed to pitch in with the arguments that there would be people—including young people— on the floats who might also be struck by coins) and partly for the silly argument that there might be a thunderstorm.

Anyway, the whole scheme collapsed for these reasons, and the Lions showed perhaps less than their usual guts in featuring a large cat for publicity instead of Marquis II. I'll bet the chap who thought up that substitution couldn't tell margarine from best butter.

Meanwhile, the Marquess of Bath was also doing his bit for

I

publicity by appearing in London's famous Selfridge's store (and being mobbed by housewives, as if he was a film star) in the company of Marquis III, Marquis II's young brother, then about four months old, and adorable. Asked how it was that there were two cubs named after Marquis in less than a year, the delightful soul said discreetly: 'The original Marquis changed his wife, y'understand. These things happen, even in the best families!'

10

A line is drawn

THE MONKEY Jungle (or Baboon Park, to name it correctly) was due to open at Whit, 1969, as an important new attraction, so, as usual, the Press was asked along a few days beforehand to have a look. Nearly two hundred and fifty baboons were to be installed in ten acres of woodland hills, next to the other parks, where they were to be allowed to swing free in the trees and roam wild generally.

'In a few years' time,' said his lordship to the reporters, absent-mindedly feeding a Bath bun to a tiny example of the breed, 'these cute little fellows will be great hairy baboons, and the females, fascinatingly, will have vividly-coloured behinds.' The other two hundred and forty-nine monkeys were still caged, ready for 'the off', having earlier had their lunch of fruit, nuts, vegetables and special vitamins. 'I'm told,' Bath ruminated, reflectively, 'that being so young and learning to grow up together, they shouldn't kill one another too much later in life, and that they will soon settle down to the rigours of the English climate which is more than I have ever done.'

'Let 'em loose, me lord,' shouted a fruity-accented groom.

The Marquess unlocked a box-cage to release the first of the baboons, which tore off pronto into the remoter regions of the nearest high tree, to watch the scene from grandstand safety. Pathetically, almost, one solitary little baboon remained in the box, studiously picking its nose and gazing enviously at his lordship's floppy red-and-white bandanna pocket handkerchief. 'Out,' ordered the sixth Marquess. 'Ouch' squeaked the baby baboon and nervously complied.

All the baboons were then released under the direction of George 'Snaky' Williams (so-called because he had previously run a snake-farm) who had been put in charge of the Monkey Jungle, and all scattered, chattering in feigned terror. Not a few made for the ten-foot high fences, with the idea of projecting themselves over, but these had been topped by slippery plastic sheets, and were totally unclimbable.

Because of the baboons' known tendency to unpredictable behaviour, and their viciously sharp little teeth, the same rules were to apply to the monkey jungle as to the lion park: windows of cars had to be kept tightly closed at all times. This precaution was based on sound principles. Baboons are extremely difficult to catch; natives go after them in the jungle and grab them by the tail to stuff them quickly into a sack; and it is a fact that at least one African was bitten for every baboon we caught.

Father had been in Kenya and Tanzania for about a year having young ones snared, and the two hundred and fifty baboons had cost him only a few pounds each, plus freight of about six pounds fifty per animal, so this was not anything like as costly a project as the others. It was, nevertheless, our third 'first' at Longleat, if you follow me. We had been first in the world with our lions; first with the largest herd of giraffe outside Africa; and now we were first with our densely-populated monkey jungle.

The baboons, by the way, are particularly partial to bananas and it's good fun to see them catching these when

'Snaky' feeds them at the appropriate times. These fluffy bound-ing-balls also dance jigs and hang upside down from car roofs, invertedly looking in the windows and gesticulating their sympathy to the 'trapped' inmates. Among the particularly wayward baboons is an older one, known as Rasputin, whose favourite game is to leap on radiators and 'adjust' windscreen-wipers. Fortunately, as in the lion reserve, no one seems to mind too much.

Baboons are very destructive creatures, back home in East Africa, where they work havoc in crops in country districts and are regarded as pests, to be wiped out, by farmers. At Longleat they are too well fed to do too much damage, although they still nibble at young leaves or any suitable berries they happen to find around their enclosure. The public is not allowed to feed them, not even through car windows, for obvious reasons.

After this new animal attraction had been added to the many already established, a jealous and up-staged rival stately-home owner was heard to mutter, re. the Chipperfields: 'What next? Griffins?'

One day, a baboon called Bobo strangled his wife in the course of a quarrel over another male monkey. He chased the would-be lover boy several times round the park and would have strangled him too, had he caught him. Instead of putting Bobo down, we allowed the laws of the jungle to operate, and it worked; he has not killed again. Instead he now uses his natural aggression to dominate a clique of monkeys in one corner of the park.

You may have wondered why the baboons squat so much on car bonnets. It's because they like the feel of the warmth of the radiator on their colourful behinds. And contrary to the old wives' tale, we haven't had one case of baboon piles.

Sadly, it was necessary to draw a line after this latest attraction had been added. On 28 May, father and the Marquess jointly announced that they had reached the limit of the Longleat complex until further notice.

However, we had had a Grant's Zebra, named 'Kenya', in the family for about ten years, and I had taught him such tricks as were needed, from time to time, in films or commercials. Now we released him with the other zebras in the East African Game Park, and, almost at once, he became a major attraction there, with one of the wardens riding him occasionally, while on patrol, as if he were a horse. Zebras are usually wild, and can be dangerous, but I had trained Kenya well, and he proved quite a pet as well as a marvellous photographic subject.

One Tuesday, three ostriches took flight and got away from the adjoining game park, whence they 'swanned' about the countryside. We had to organise a round-up at once, not because they are dangerous but because they can travel for considerable distances at up to forty miles per hour. Indeed, we had to chase them all the way to Frome before we got in front and rounded them up.

I still wonder what the villagers thought *en route* when they looked out of their windows, to see the trio of giant birds in full flight, line ahead like the carriages of an express train, pursued by garishly dressed 'white hunters' in gaudily painted safari trucks in the midst of rural England. But maybe by now they had got to know about 'they mad folk up at the estate an' their wild animiles.'

Just after Whit, we opened our first fifty-fifty deal in Australia —a lion park of forty-five animals in a hundred acres at Warragamba, forty miles south-west of Sydney. Known as African Lion Safari, it cost two hundred thousand pounds to set up. Partners with my father in this case, were my brother Richard; Major Geoffrey Gibbon, a British licensed hunter and a bachelor; and Mr. Alfred Bullen, of the well-known Australian circus family.

Essentially the same ground-rules were laid down there as here, with the same sort of fences (two miles of them); the same winding road (three miles); the same control conditions, wardens, radio links, children's corner, and so on.

Other major Chipperfield moves were afoot at this point in time, the chief one being that the very rich Earl of Derby— fifty-one years of age, and very much a pillar of the Establishment for most of his life—had now made his mind up to get into the Stately Home act, under my father's guidance. An announcement was made, just before Christmas, that they would jointly spend a million pounds or more turning several hundred acres of the grounds of fabled Knowsley Hall, near Liverpool, into a wild-animal reserve. In so doing, the Earl would appear to be defying in rather a big way, his famous family's motto, which is 'Without Changing'. Up to this point, Lord Derby had not been involved in the Stately Homes' Stakes, and had not even let the public into the Hall regularly for about ten years. Now, it seemed, he was going the whole way.

Undoubtedly, part of the reason for this move—and for the equally-dramatic one made earlier by the dominant Duke of Bedford—was the fact that our pioneering at Longleat had cleared the air of a lot of misapprehensions about lions—those symbols of the character we Britons used to think we had.

When we first opened the reserve (could it really be as long ago as 1966?) there had been leaders in *The Times*, questions in Parliament, and local resistance groups galore. Now, as my brother Richard prepared for the impending opening of Woburn's Wild Animal Kingdom, with something like a million pounds' worth of animals, including lions galore, the event was treated as casually as if it were a newly-opened R.S.P.C.A. cat-home or a hatchery for freshwater fish.

This is all to the good. In the main, it was the 'professional' complainers—the writers of letters to the editor; the publicity-seeking politicians; the cranks, and such like, who had made our lives miserable for months in 1966. The general public had showed itself to be much wiser, by flocking in thousands either

to see our magnificent and intelligent beasts in natural surround-
ings, or else to see how many spectators would be eaten alive
in the first few weeks! What had started as a twinkle in my father's
eye had quickly become big—some say *roaring* business. Indeed,
about the same time as Woburn, we would be opening another
prestigious and potentially *very* profitable venture on similar
lines in Baronet Sir John Muir's estate at Blairdrummond, near
Doune, Stirlingshire.

Lions in stately homesteads are now very much here to stay.
We have not increased the numbers greatly in the reserve at
Longleat, because fifty was a figure carefully chosen to suit the
size and style of the lion park. But we have produced lots of
cubs there—averaging about thirty births per year, each worth
three to four hundred pounds—and we have exported some and
imported others, to prevent in-breeding and towards the establishment of the best strain of lions in the world. As the average
lion lives to about thirty, in conditions of non-aggression, we
are certainly preparing well for the future.

Among the most successful of the original mothers in the lion
park at Longleat were Nella and Racer, lionesses from Stockholm,
who had just produced their second litters of four and three lions
respectively and were rearing them with fiercely affectionate skill.
They were automatically marked out in our minds as key figures,
with Marquis, Lady and Countess, in lion-breeding plans.

We had been equally thrilled, in recent weeks, by the fact that
the breeding cycle had begun, sooner than we could have dared
to hope, in the giraffe community at Longleat. It is more difficult
to judge the mating than with lions because it is complicated by
the fact that the male giraffe comes into season, like the female,
and when these periods coincide, they both become a bit like the
mad March hare, and have to be watched.

We started with a tragedy, when the first giraffe mother, alas,
deliberately kicked her baby to death, presumably because she

detected some weakness in it we could not discern. And when the second mother had an accident with one of her twins we crossed ourselves more vigorously than usual. She had appeared to be an excellent mother, nuzzling her two babies on to their spindly legs, in copybook manner, and guiding their first tentative steps. But after a few minutes, in trying to keep her own feet, she, too kicked a baby, albeit accidentally, and he collapsed on the grass like a house made of matches. She then nuzzled him on the ground for a while, puzzling why he did not get up. Eventually, she gave up and took the other calf off to join 'father', leaving the injured one where he was.

We quickly stepped in at this point, and, after a quick look at the little fellow, called the vet, who confirmed that the baby giraffe had a dislocated hip. This was quickly set and he was isolated, with his mother and brother, until he was fit and well again. After this, there had been no accidents, I am very pleased to say.

The same vet had a lengthier problem the same week in the same park, when one of the adult giraffes, a four-year-old, named Caroline, stuck her neck out and developed the longest sore throat of the year. It was external, fortunately. She had hurt herself on a passing tree while trying to reach some new young shoots at the top. Her sixteen-foot height gave the vet a pain in the neck at first, as he tried to reach the wound. But we coaxed her into a crate, to keep her still, and then rigged up a special platform for the vet, where he was able to confirm that bandages were needed. Ordinary ones would not do, so we improvised again, and I dug out some yards of extra-wide material normally used for wrapping the legs of my horses.

Altogether, it was quite a week for accidents. On the Saturday, David fell and broke his right leg. He was getting on for four and very strong. It was a simple fall, leading to quite a complicated fracture, as these things often do. But he took it bravely and nobody bothered very much, except his friend Charles, the chimp.

Charles was apparently absolutely inconsolable about the accident until I happened to read his expression and analyse his anguish. One morning, when I had a moment to spare, I improvised a splint, bandages and plaster for Charles's right leg, exactly the same as David's. Thereafter, all was bliss, as they hobbled around together with mournful glee. At least, all was bliss until David's crutches arrived! Then it was murder again, (with Charles forever stealing David's props and loping expertly away) until a similar small pair had been got for Charles. And for the six weeks or so it took for David's leg to heal, they lived happily together again, hobbling around like a couple of little old men and lapping up any sympathy they could get from other animals and people!

Charles has long been convinced he is David's brother. Reared in the family, he identifies entirely with the human race. He clutches at me, like babies do, when he's scared. Games in which lips are smacked, or backing-up is part of the rules, leading with the bottom, are his favourites. Like all chimps, he is also polite and, when called, to tea or, equally, for a telling-off, will advance meekly with downcast eyes. Charles greatly enjoys travelling by car, and it is hard to resist his appeals when he knows we are going on a journey. The trouble is that once he is let out *en route* to do his 'numbers' (whether 'number one' or 'number two') it quite often proved difficult to persuade him to return to the car, if there were birds to chase or rabbit holes to investigate. The easiest way we found was to send David to fetch him back.

Charles can escape from almost anything or anywhere. We've often thought if we go broke we'll employ him, Fagan-like, to break into banks and steal for us. The padlock has not been invented that he cannot pick. It takes him a little time, but he can always make it in the end. When he's a nuisance, Roger puts him out in the garden, padlocked to a gate or a fence. Sure as sure, within an hour, Charles will appear at the kitchen door, grinning his diabolical grin, the open padlock in his hands. He does it by scratching about in the garden until he finds bits of wire or nails suitable for the job. Sometimes when we notice what he's up to, Roger pops out and gives him an apple to take his mind off the padlock, and this usually means the shackle last half-an-hour longer.

Another fascinating aspect of the chimp's character is his jealousy. Occasionally, Roger will throw a punch at me in fun and pretend to smack me. This drives Charles absolutely insane, especially if I pretend to cry. He jumps up and down, pulls at the hair on top of his head, and grunts aggressively at Roger. Then if I say, 'Kiss me better, Charles,' he comes over and puts his arms round my neck and offers his big lips up in a kiss; then all is well again. But if Roger is ever murdered, which God forbid, it won't be the butler who 'done' it; it will either be Charles the chimp or Marquis the lion.

David, on the other hand, can take me or leave me. We're very good pals, but he doesn't actually need me all that much—which is a good thing in a boy. He weighed nine pounds when he was born, having kicked me vigorously for what seemed like months beforehand (and I write this with the more feeling because I was again pregnant in the summer of 1970, and it's the wrong time to be carrying a baby, if you're as active as I have to be, when the weather is hot) and he's still as strong as any of the young animals he plays with.

He takes it all for granted—the exotic life he leads, compared to other children; indeed he is lost only if we take him somewhere where there are no animals. He finds other children boring by comparison with chimps, cubs and dogs. He has been bitten by more types of animal (including snakes, tigers, leopards, panthers and crocodiles) than almost anyone, except his mum!

Indeed, they have a card for him at Warminster Hospital. Over the years, 'casualty' entries on it have run the gauntlet from 'bitten by a lion' to 'kicked by a zebra'. He recently had to go along because he had acidentally damaged a bone in his foot. 'What's the tall story this time?' asked the doctor. 'I suppose an elephant trampled on you, eh?'

Old enemies and new horizons

THERE WERE
still plenty of critics around at the time the four-hundred-acre
Wild Animal Kingdom opened at Woburn in May, 1970, but they
had re-orchestrated their theme. Now we were overdoing things,
and would put ourselves out of business that way; sure, a few
lions in the open was fine (had not they always said so?) but with
hundreds of them around, people would get bored. Besides, the
competition from all the new reserves we were now opening
would siphon off so much traffic from Longleat that Lord Bath
would probably throw Jimmy Chipperfield to his damned lions—
so ran the new pontifications of the pundits.

The truth was that not only was the competition proving good
for Longleat, but that also public demand for the sort of exotic
'shows' we were putting on appeared to be insatiable.

Those arch-rivals, the Marquess of Bath and the Duke of
Bedford, indeed, saw so clearly that there was ample cake for both
that the former was man enough to perform the opening ceremony
at Woburn, and the latter had stature enough to make this
splendid gesture of unity, if not of friendship.

'I know we are cut-throat competitors, strictly speaking, but at the rate the Duke attracts tourists, I have no doubt he will lick the pants off us in no time', Bath generously and courteously told the Press. 'Everything he touches seems to turn to gold.'

The animals, however, were less well-behaved than the stately-home owners. As Lord Bath cut the blue ribbon, three baby elephants charged at him, and one of them (Tess by name) tried out her weight of four hundred and fifty pounds on his foot. Later as the Marquess drove around the park (said to be the largest outside Africa) in his Bentley, a lion named Reggie leaped on to the hood. 'I wonder if he'll sit there while I drive him down to Longleat,' his lordship pondered, seeing not a lion, but a till ringing up a three-hundred-and-fifty-pound bonus.

This was all very jolly and cosy, but it was already evident that there were good defensive and commercial reasons for a linking of arms, because father, the Marquess and the Duke had prodded to fury a common enemy, in the corporate, collective sense. The opening of the Wild Animal Kingdom, in particular, had raised a larger-than-ever amount of ire in exalted quarters, standing as it did a catapulted-ripe-egg throw away from the country branch (at Whipsnade) of London Zoo. Longleat had long been taking business away from London, but the fact was partly clouded by distance; the new reserve would now be seen to hurt Whipsnade, and that really demanded action from zoological stuffed-shirts, one and all.

There are many compensations for the sacrifices we have made in settling down with the animals at Longleat; the dusty downs of Wiltshire, for instance; the white elder-blossom, and dog-roses hanging in the hedges. I adore the high and sulky weather we get in the south-west and the long evening shadows, pointing to folded villages, with their homing cows and after-church walkers. I love the way darkness comes to The Pheasantry—wood smoke, camphor and animal warmth, contrasting with the velvety emptiness of the night world outside, with brilliant but cold stars over, and later to be put to sleep to the gentle stirrings of beasts at rest.

Nobody could lead a busier life, and yet, here, in one of the most ancient Kingdoms of England there is still time—time to watch a man herding sheep in a side road, or boiling a can of spring water (an hour it could take) to make an incomparable pot of tea.

Wiltshire has its plague of motor-cars, trying to cut the landscape to pieces, and as we live by them, we should not complain, but fortunately most of it is not yet bulldozed for speed. Many of the country roads still follow their original 'English drunkard' routes, once followed by packhorse and the lumbering cartwheel, etched tracks that hug the curve of a valley or yield to a promontory, like the wandering line of a stream, amid vast and rolling plains, covered with shaggy grass which looks as though cropped by mammoths.

Somehow I still contrive time occasionally to take in market day, and the town square crowded with bone-thin sheep; with farmers standing around to gossip, talking sideways to one another and all looking in opposite directions, like figures in a waxworks, and contrasting with animated dealers counting out crumpled money as they burst on to pavements from open-all-day pubs, while shepherds and their dogs sit around on the kerbs, longing to be back in the Mendip hills.

These are some of the things I have retained, or gained, through the Longleat safari scheme; they are bonuses of incomparable value, but they are just part of a natural scheme of things the open-park animal world offers that no zoo (however imaginatively created) can ever give.

Personally, I feel no great sympathy for the position into which we have thrown the established zoological groups, from whom we are rapidly taking business hand over hand—particularly the London one. Despite the worthy efforts of Sir Solly Zuckerman and others, the vast sums the London Zoological Society has been given or loaned do not, in my view, make it more efficient or modern-minded. Indeed, the competition the 'safari parks' have provided, almost single-handed, in recent years, may turn out to be the best thing that ever happened to the Society. Chipperfield standards are every bit as high as theirs, and we are able confidently to plough millions into successful development. 'Nationalised' organisations almost always go soft and become overstaffed. We have to succeed, and, therefore, we know where we are going, how and why. But we also know our animals from the heart as well as from the brain. It's 'in our blood' as they say.

Man cannot, try as he likes, separate himself from the rest of his fellow creatures. An elephant is as important to life in its fashion as an ant; a sparrow as an eagle: all play their parts on the world stage alongside man. We are certainly not the last word. They were here before us. Some of them at least may be here long after we have destroyed ourselves. I learn very little from people, but I learn new things every day from my animals. Marquis has taken a lot from me in time and energy, but he has given me back so much that I can only repay it by going on and on repeating the experiences, the experiments with other wild creatures.

Wild animals are big business in Britain today, but mainly in our sector. Indeed, wild-life parks are the fastest growing sector of the entertainment business—more than justifying father's decision to get out of the circus when the public no longer wanted it and into the pioneering of animals in parks, which the public did want, more and more. Of course, that does not mean we shall not also become involved again in circuses, if the tide should turn that way. Habit is strong in the Chipperfield clan.

But, as I say, we had certainly shaken up the traditionalists, and now they had switched from talk to action. It may, indeed, be interesting to recall, in this context, that, in an account dating back as far as 1929, Zuckerman produced a classical study of a large colony of hamadryad baboons at the London Zoo, which told of thirty-three deaths among the females (of which all but three were from fighting), and of five youngsters born in the cage all dying of wounds. Modern-minded zoologists, of course (and I do not exclude Sir Solly) accept that the major cause of neurosis among wild animals is being shut up behind bars and deprived of following their normal patterns of behaviour. To make a point, by admittedly over-simplifying the matter, why do not the zoological societies do like us, remove their bars, their concrete walls and their blocks of offices, and move out into the free countryside, together with their animals?

Anyway, as I say, at least we had goaded them from words to action. No sooner had the first six rare white rhinos (which are really parchment coloured, by the way, even if you wash them with Tide) settled in at Woburn than it was announced that the London Zoological Society had become the sole European agency for white rhino, which it had previously helped to preserve at Whipsnade. In April 1970 my father made an attempt to purchase through them three more pairs of white rhinos for Woburn, three for a new breeding colony at Longleat and eight pairs for other Game Reserves, but he was told that the rhinos available from Natal that year were committed for orders already negotiated. These included the Society's new herd at Whipsnade, other European orders and orders for collections outside Europe. Our plans had to be shelved.

This led to a fear that, having set a precedent over the white rhino (which had been galloping towards complete extinction in Africa, partly because of an erroneous belief that the beast's powdered horn is a powerful aphrodisiac) the London Zoological Society might somehow use their long-established international connections to restrict distribution of other rare breeds. If this happened, it could prove the thin end of the wedge, in so far as stocking up wild-life parks is concerned, and, tragically, could

K

hold back the conservation of such species in which we have become deeply involved. Sooner or later, it now seemed to me, London Zoo may go even further by grabbing more and more sole agencies, thereby controlling our expansion and depriving us of animals even though we have vastly better facilities for breeding and building herds than they have. To us, indeed, it looked very much like a deliberate move to stifle competition—*our* competition —because we were more successful and were taking away customers.

There have been charges that we put less back than do the traditional zoos. This is the uttermost nonsense. Not only does our money go back into animals, in exporting as well as importing (in research, breeding, restocking and ringing the changes) but we finance experiments here and abroad, the better to care for and conserve animals.

Diet, for example, is one of our chief concerns. And at an early stage of establishing our wild life parks, my father sent out his own team of scientists to Africa to gather grasses, bushes, trees and any other flora the native fauna lives off. These were brought home and analysed—hundreds of tests being carried out on each.

As a result, we have encouraged a firm in Britain to produce a special concentrate, in pellet form. The firm is Spillers (in the personage of an extremely helpful marketing executive, Winston Rowe); through our discussions on giraffes and exotic animals, quantities of carefully-boosted horse-cubes for such creatures were produced and supplied especially for us.

Even the drinking-water in the wild was put to the test and compared with what was available in the reserves here. Research also taught us that carefully-judged quantities of bone-meal sprinkled on the ox-heads daily fed to the lions increased their strength and virility. Their main dishes are also doused with cod-liver oil, to keep the cold out and to give healthy snugness to their winter coats.

The fruits of all this early research can now be seen in the splendid coats *all* our wild animals possess, from marmalade lions' fur to mottled giraffe silk, as well as in the remarkable successes we are chalking up in breeding from even the most difficult of animals.

We also ring the changes as we can. Bedford has his rare white rhino. In addition to all the usual animals, Lord Derby (whose million-pound park would open in July, 1971, and would also become an instant *succes fou*) would have cheetahs (like the white rhino, on the extinction list) and rare antelopes (the greater Kudu). Sir John Muir, as well as his lion reserve and full range of African animals, had been packing in the visitors with the only comprehensive safari park in Scotland, where our biggest problem to date lay in getting the giraffes it features to Stirlingshire from Plymouth without taking them under any bridges that would snap off their slender necks! There are also plans for special attractions in our planned park south of Newcastle upon Tyne, and ventures are in the pipeline in five new countries overseas.

In short, the successes, since 1966, have been staggering. In particular, just as Longleat was the 'first' of the wild-life complexes, it did not take long for Woburn to establish itself as the biggest. Apart from the range and numbers of the animals featured—including five elephants, the six white rhino (each worth as much as a Rolls Royce), twenty wildebeest, twenty-two giraffes, eleven zebra, fifteen elands, three oryx, three waterbucks, fifty lions, a hundred baboons, twenty bison, nine sea-lions, a hippo and twenty crown cranes—it attracted visitors from the first day as if it was giving away pound notes, instead of taking them from every car at the turnstiles.

In fact, by the end of the 1970 season, Woburn was pulling in visitors at a rate of over two-and-a-half million per year—more even than London Zoo—which could only clock one-and-three-quarter million (with Whipsnade, under 'the same management', adding less than half-a-million) and even better results are expected there as well as at Knowsley. In Britain, indeed, the grand total of annual visitors to Chipperfield-inspired reserves is climbing rapidly towards ten million per annum. It passed eight million by early 1971.

All the main wild animal 'stately' reserves in Britain and abroad began as fifty-fifty deals between my father and each estate owner, and although one or two overseas ones were sold off because of quarantine difficulties, most are still in the family. This may seem like something of a monopoly, but it has been shown to work very well, the more so in view of the Chipperfields' almost unique expertise.

Although I have played down the accident factor, it is important to remember that none of our animals in any of the estates has lost the killer instinct. Lions, for instance, are blessed with the ability to observe while remaining absolutely still, and as you watch a pride apparently asleep at Longleat or Woburn or elsewhere, it may well be that they are watching *you*, for tell-tale movements, in your role as possible prey. In addition, they have absolutely no fear; they will always investigate anything unusual, in or out of the cars they have become semi-accustomed to, such as trailing ropes, waving hands and whiplashing aerials. Any such thing may galvanise a big cat to sudden, fast, unpredictable impulses. People behind windows do not interest them (unless the windows are open, even slightly) and, generally speaking, they avoid adults even outside cars (although this, too, is an unpredictable factor and certainly not a rule), but please *always* remember that children are regarded by lions as quick and easy prey.

We have made all our reserves completely safe, as long as no-one breaks the rules about keeping car doors and windows closed (and sounding the horn in case of breakdown). Insurance was extremely difficult to arrange before Longleat opened, but now brokers are falling over themselves to get our business. In all cases, we insure against accidents for up to two hundred and fifty thousand pounds per person should we be held responsible. World-wide, our turnstiles had clicked away to the tune of over ten million visitors in the first four years. And accidents have been rare to the point that they are not even statistics.

There was one case at Woburn, in the summer of 1970 (the first accident involving injury to a visitor in any of our parks), of a little five-year-old girl who was mauled by a lioness named Twiggy, who had thrust her head through the open car-window and tried to drag the child from its mother's arms. This was serious enough, but not, thank God, fatal or near it. It would not have happened at all if the family had kept the window shut as is the rule for the park. One interesting point we were able to put over to the public and the Press over this was that Twiggy did not have to be 'put down' as a result. Richard locked her away for a few days in solitary confinement, but rather because it was expected of him than for any other reason. There is no truth whatsoever in the old-wives' tale that lions, having once tasted human blood, are crazy for more. Nor do their mental processes operate in a way that enables them to 'remember' that there is flesh and blood behind the glass windows of the cars they see every day.

Twiggy showed no interest in any cars after the accident, although she was roaming free in the park for the rest of the day. And she, herself, became a mother a few weeks later, so who's to say what her feelings were during the earlier incident? Eventually, she rejected her one cub, Muki, but that is far from unusual, as I have tried to show, since Marquis the First and the Second were both rejected. Muki, by the way, is Swahili for girl. The world-figure for total attendances at our reserves had reached nine million at the time of the sole accident, and as father said: 'Not only was this not in any way our fault, but also you could not take nine million people across the road without killing half-a-dozen of them. As a day out, lion-watching is much safer than, say, sailing. And provided everyone obeys the instructions, it is no more dangerous than watching TV.'

Alas, despite the warning, despite the 'white hunters', despite the notices every few yards, people still got out of their cars at all our reserves for the silliest reasons, and literally dozens have diced with death over the years, *all* owing their lives to the alertness and courage of our wardens—these marvellous men, with the yard-long swagger sticks, who have the enthusiasm of men whose work is still stimulatingly fresh to them. It is a continuing problem, but short of putting a 'white hunter' in every car, I do not see what more we can do than we are doing to ensure safety. We have had complaints that our men are too strict and some visitors find them officious. But all I can say is that if I ever found a warden who was really *popular* with the public, I'd sack him.

Although we are taking fantastic sums of money, as if we were holding successful pop concerts every day, if you like, and think nothing of having to count a large number of pound notes at Longleat on a Sunday; although we already have more lions on show than Ethiopia, and will soon have more than Kenya; although even feeding the lions with ox-heads at about seventy-five pence a throw (apart altogether from feeding the more choosy creatures) has made rich men out of knackermen, from Scotland to Cornwall, we have not in any way changed our life-style.

What I'm trying to say is that we go on growing and succeeding because we believe in doing thrifty but sensible deals, and in ploughing back every farthing we can spare. We feel truly rich, for example, because we now own more than a hundred giraffes, which is something I don't believe anyone else in the animal world can say. And with at least a tenth of these due to calve soon (which could never have happened in any zoos) we are going to be richer still, in the best sense.

There are always worries, of course, with animals as well as with the public, and some are quite as unpredictable as they are frightening when they happen. Richard, for instance, ran into an unheard-of problem at Woburn, in the severe weather at Christmas, 1970. Although the public was still rolling through the gates in astonishing numbers (despite bitter conditions) and were looking forward to seeing the twenty-two giraffes just as much as the fifty lions, they had to be content with the latter. As soon as the metalled roads in the park (which are a feature in the picnic area at Woburn) iced up, the giraffes began involuntarily executing the splits. This was something we had never encountered before, but it would have been silly to risk injuring them, so the entire herd had to be shut in their heated loose-boxes until the weather improved. Meanwhile, father soon had our expert working out which type of new road-surface would be safest for the waltzing cloven-hooved feet of a herd of Ugandan giraffes.

Another worry (this time at Longleat) was that Paleface, a frisky five-year-old giraffe, who had waited fourteen long months for the arrival of her first baby, lost it, only days after the calf was born, when it dropped dead from natural causes. Paleface, normally chirpy, became fretful—a morose and moody 'loner' in the game park. Then, one day, Roger had an idea. David had acquired a six-foot-high toy giraffe, called Spotty, at Christmas and was bored with it. So we presented Spotty to Paleface, to see what would happen. Sure enough, Paleface nuzzled its foam rubber body and she licked it all over. She seemed to draw comfort from its presence in her quarters. So much so that, in a few days, she was herself again and rejoined the other seventeen giraffes in the herd.

Maybe I'm making it sound easy and romantic, as well as profitable. If so, let me firmly correct any such impressions. Wild animals are not for amateurs. I cannot state this fact too often or too strongly. I am a full-time professional, and therefore everything I do with animals is based on experience backed by shrewdly acquired kno\ ledge. It may *seem* simple and soppy. In truth, it is so deadly seriou. that I have to be alert and watchful every second, even with Marqu ` and his sons. You can never, never, never go all the way with a v wild animal and trust it completely. Any such animal, of any s̨ ·cies, can turn on the one it 'loves' suddenly coldly, viciously and, bove all, unpredictably. Who is to say which of a hundred reaso̱ ʒ are behind such an action? The fact is, it can happen without w̱ ·ning. You can never guess when a sudden urge to kill will overc̱ me all other instincts.

So, no matter how affectionat̞ ·ly inclined I may be to an animal friend, I see to it that I *never* get ̓n a position of physical vulnerability. The training of wild anima's, in particular, is exclusively for professionals; no amateur can lea̱ ʏ it all, learn it thoroughly, and maintain the disciplines required t̩ keep it up, day after day, night after night, for as long as he or s̩ ʒ and the animals shall live together.

That even professionals can slip up, in a m̩ ʼment of temporary unwatchfulness, was to be underlined tragica'v in July, 1971, when a head ranger at Woburn would be killed by an eland bull-antelope (of all things)—a beast with which he had been on the most excellent terms for months. If this can happen to a fully-trained, careful and highly experienced professional, how can a part-time dabbler hope to survive?

Alas, we have an unfortunate situation in Britain, which those of us who know the rules and the dangers are concerned about, and would like to see changed—if only this can be legislated for in the *right* way, by providing necessary safeguards without imposing unnecessary restrictions on freedom.

The problem is that, the way things are, nobody can say how many non-domestic animals, and of what species, are being kept as 'pets', because it is not required by law that anybody should be told. No licence is needed to buy wild animals, or to keep them (except, curiously, for great apes, kangaroos, wallabies and rhinos

—*not* the most sought-after of pets, I'd guess). And, unless they are hooved animals, monkeys, or of the dog and cat families, they do not even have to serve a 'sentence' in quarantine. Up to a point, such freedoms are good in a democracy, but the situation wants watching.

Another, perhaps more disturbing fact is that anyone can call his or her collection a zoo, or a zoo farm, and let the public in to see it without any authority knowing. As I mentioned, again nobody knows the true numbers, but it is believed that such places are being opened at a rate of about thirty per year. There is not even any obligation on the local police to see that the 'inmates' are securely caged. Inevitably, in many cases it soon proves necessary for the R.S.P.C.A. to attack the owners, as best it can, for the poor and unsafe conditions in which the animals are kept.

A monkey, which can pass on a fatal brain disease to humans (a form of encephalitis, of which the virus is the most deadly known to man) is anything but a cuddly toy. A nine-inch alligator may seem a fascinating pet, but what happens when it grows to a snapping monster of three feet or more? Bear cubs are enchanting, but when they grow up they become the world's most vicious and least trustworthy animals—some black bears also growing until they weigh four hundred pounds at seven feet. Bears are cunning enough to be prone to escape, and can cause the most frightful injuries. An average-sized chimp could bite your hand off. Baboons' teeth can tear your flesh to ribbons.

When I hear of wolves in a London backyard, alligators in the stockbroker belt of Surrey, bears in a midland garage, and an elephant in a stable in Welwyn Garden City, l cringe for the animals and for the neighbours. At a calmer level, too, I wonder how many eager but ignorant would-be pet-owners realise that a bush-baby needs to sleep all day, that badgers need a concrete enclosure, or that an otter needs a stream to play in, and at least three pounds of whiting per day.

In a sentence, a large number of potential killers in Britain are totally outside the law. It is perfectly all right to keep lions, tigers, boa-constrictors, orang-utangs, hyenas and such like, but heaven help you if you want to set up a boarding-house for a few domestic cats; government inspectors will want to know all about it. Isn't it time the appropriate laws were looked at sensibly?

As I mentioned, we keep a book listing 'incidents' which involve wild animals, and which are reported to us by the police or other authorities, just in case we are blamed for any of them; and here is a random selection from the many the book held by this time—covering a period of from two to three years:

Two alligators (male and female) of adult size, released into the Grand Union Canal near Leicester and never found. Are they breeding, I wonder? Actually, they are unlikely to have survived the first spell of frost, but it makes you wonder, all the same, what has happened to them!

Lioness reported seen several times in Epping Forest, but never found; a cheetah or leopard often observed in south London and north Kent, and hunted without success; a 'ferocious' animal with snapping jaws seen but never located in Gloucester; two Australian dingoes, which attacked a child at Derby, were fortunately recaptured; a dangerous monkey was caught after trying to savage several people at Biggin Hill; a three-ton elephant, roaming Paignton, Devon, was eventually captured; two gorillas terrorised villagers at Bekesbourne, before being recaptured; a tiger was hunted by police in Norfolk but was never found; a pet bear mauled a baroness in Suffolk and was shot by the baron; wolves in several places were shot and killed; a puma kept appearing and disappearing in Hampshire, Sussex and Surrey, but was never pinned down; a tiger was chased by police at Lyndhurst, Hampshire (*not* one of ours, although in our general area) but got away, never to be seen again; another pet bear killed a boy at Thurrock, Essex and was killed in turn by the boy's father; and lion tracks were reported (and confirmed) near Wigan, but the lion that made them was never seen and never found.

I could go on and on, but these are typical of a curious and continuing situation, partly brought about by the fact that anyone can keep almost any number of assorted wild animals around their home if they feel so inclined, without let or hindrance; there is no law against such anti-social and dangerous conduct, although quite a lot of us think there should be.

On the other side of the coin, I am bound to explain that there *are* legal obligations on the owners of wild animals, the most important of which is that he or she must, as an absolute duty, try to prevent them from escaping. There is attendant liability for injury or damage should one or more escape, whether it was the owner's fault or was due to someone else's negligence. And if an escaped wild animal manages to stay at liberty for years, its owner's liability for its actions can still hold.

But the law is not so straightforward in the case of injury or damage caused by a person's wild animals on his own property. If notices are put up warning any lawful visitors of the dangers, or if they are informed by word of mouth, the owner would not be liable if any such injury or damage resulted. Both these methods of warning are employed at Longleat.

Trespassers are another matter, again. In general, if a person is attacked by an animal while trespassing, it is considered to be his own fault. Woe betide, therefore, the burglar who tries to break into The Pheasantry. If the dogs did not get him, then the lion, or tigers or black panther, or pythons, or some other such creature might. And if he lived to tell the tale, that would be all he would get out of it.

We have to be careful, however, to warn tradesmen and all other visitors to the house, because even trained or docile animals can get their owners into trouble the way the law stands. A few of my women friends have an unnatural fear of snakes, some of which I sometimes have around the office or the sitting-room. And the law says that if I suddenly produce a grass snake, or something harmless like that, and the sight of it gives someone a bad fright, the victim (unless warned) might gain damages from me.

As far as our domestic animals (or anyone's) are concerned, the law in England is extremely tolerant. If a dog or a cat, or some such attacks anyone, its owner will not be held liable unless it can be proved that he knew it was in danger of doing this. Proof is generally deemed to have been laid if the animal has attacked, or attempted to attack, someone previously.

The definition of a domestic animal, however, is so loose that if someone was suddenly bitten by an Arabian camel in my back-yard (a not-impossible happening!) they would stand very little chance of gaining damages, whereas, if it had been a giraffe that attacked, without warning, damages might be awarded. The law considers the Arabian camel to be a domestic beast (since no-where is it found truly wild) and the giraffe (because it has no function other than to be in the wild) is considered to be a danger-ous wild animal in the matter of doing damage or conferring injury.

The English law being such an ass, where it applies to animals, as elsewhere, there are one or two other contrary twists to look out for. Cats may kill fancied pigeons, for instance, at considerable cost to the fanciers, but it would be most unlikely if the latter's claims to damages succeeded. On the other hand, a special Act of Parliament was introduced some years ago to ensure that, if a dog attacks poultry or cattle, you can find yourself liable for appropriate and possibly costly damages.

Again, on the other hand, both cats and dogs are considered by the law to have 'a natural propensity to stray'. So if a neighbour's cat or dog wanders on to your land and does damage, you are most unlikely to be able to obtain redress, although 'nuisance' can be proved if the habit continues after warnings.

Cats can cause motor accidents and their owners will probably get off scot-free. But if a dog acts in exactly the same way, negligence by the owner can often be proved. Dog-owners can also be blamed if their pets cause accidents to pedestrians.

In the law, the term 'cattle' can mean sheep and chickens as well as cows, bulls and horses, and again there are anomalies. Your cattle can wander into a road and cause an accident and you will not be liable; but if they get through a fence, which is your responsibility, and stray on to a neighbour's land, he can generally win an action against you. It is a curious quirk, indeed, that although you must maintain fences on to neighbouring land with diligence, it is not an obligation to fence off your cattle from the highway.

Noise nuisance (equally from pets, or cattle, or wild animals) can take any of us into court where we can be ordered to abate the noise. Fortunately, at Longleat and at The Pheasantry, neighbours are few and far between, but we are always watchful, none the less.

Please don't be cruel to animals (apart altogether from maybe getting innocent blood on your hands therefrom) by thinking that animal training is a matter of knowing that goats will come to you for a piece of peppermint: that turkeys will gobble in response to a high-pitched whistle; or that macaws will stay put wherever you tell them to. It is perhaps the most dedicated profession there is. By all means, go into it as a career (as long as you know that the apprenticeship will be long, wearisome and painstaking). I'm not a spoilsport, but do not, I pray you, under any circumstances, *dabble* in the keeping and training of non-domestic animals. Too often, it can mean an unpleasant death for them and death or maiming for you or for your loved ones or for strangers. It's just not worth it. The world's a miserable enough place for animals and humans without making it worse.

You may ask how it is one person gets on much better with animals than another. Really, I'm just about the last person in the world capable of replying, because, from babyhood, it has just come naturally to me. If I say it's because I smell right, I'm probably as near the mark as if I say it is because of some personal magnetism I possess. The truth is, no one knows for sure; it just happens that way. I couldn't paint a picture, or write a symphony, if I studied twelve hours a day for fifty years. But I can teach almost any trick to any animal, given a few weeks to work at it.

Let me end with two short tales that maybe sum up what relationships between wild animals and human beings are about. One day, when Marquis was four-and-a-half—a magnificent specimen, tall as a Shetland pony and muscled like an Olympic weight-lifter—I still had him around the house most of the time. And one afternoon when we were practising some tricks in a large room at the back of The Pheasantry, a little rhesus monkey got in through the small open window. Someone had been transferring the monkey from one crate to another outside, and it had seen what it thought was a way to escape. Instead, it landed on the floor a few feet from my overgrown ginger mog and pandemonium broke loose like never before.

If medium-sized Marquis was scared of the robin earlier, large Marquis was absolutely petrified at the monkey now. And if robin had been swift to get out of the way of the lion's paws, the little chattering fellow was infinitely quicker.

Whizz! Bang! Wallop! Zoom! It reminded me of a scene from a speeded-up animated cartoon. Round and round they went; up and down they went, and Marquis never came within a foot of clouting the enemy. It was Jack Bodell taking on Ken Buchanan. The monkey flew like a butterfly and leapt like a grasshopper, with the lion floundering around in an agony of fear. At last, bursting with laughter, I managed to catch the little fellow in my arms, while talking calming words to Marquis, who had got himself into such a condition of dust and sweat he looked more like a tatty old stuffed rug than the King of anywhere. 'You smell like the tom-cat from next door,' I laughed to the trembling giant, when the circus was over. 'Come and have a swim in the pond.'

The very next day, the Press were down by invitation, taking general pictures, as they do from time to time, and one of the shots I set up for them was of Marquis standing nobly at the top of the steps in front of Longleat House, looking thoroughly dyed-in-the-ermine.

It was a marvellous subject for a picture, and the photographers were crowded round banging away, while Roger and I stood by, at the foot of the steps, blushing soppily, like proud parents, at the compliments being thrown at us, while watching Marquis all the time lest he misbehave. In fact he was perfect, holding his pose for two or three minutes (as I had asked him to do) and I was ready to climb the steps to put him on his chain for the walk home. At that precise moment there was a bang, a flash and a wallop. A photographer's bulb had burst; Marquis had leapt forward in fear; and Roger was lying on the ground with a four-hundred-pound lion on top of him.

It was nobody's fault, but the accident (which could have killed my beloved husband, but only bruised him) taught me a lesson I had been avoiding. I had kept a lion as a friend for a fairly long part of his lifetime. Now, as my wise father had been trying to tell me for a long time, I was being rather silly to try to extend the span any longer. I cried as I led my lion back to The Pheasantry for the very last time, and even my new baby daughter, Suzanne, was hushed at the sight of me. The next day, Marquis, his sons, and his wives were taken off to a new freedom in a reserve where they would be unlikely to see me often. Back at the 'orphanage', I jumped horses around the paddock until I was tired enough to sleep and not to fret.